HI-TECH TRAINS

HI-TECH TRAINS

THE ULTIMATE IN SPEED, POWER AND STYLE

ARTHUR TAYLER

THE
APPLE
PRESS

A QUINTET BOOK

Published by The Apple Press
6 Blundell Street
London N7 9BH

ISBN 1-85076-397-6

This book was designed and produced by
Quintet Publishing Limited
6 Blundell Street
London N7 9BH

Creative Director: Richard Dewing
Designer: Stuart Walden
Project Editor: Damian Thompson
Editor: John O.E. Clark
Picture Researchers:
Damian Thompson and Mirco De Cet
Illustrator: Danny McBride

Typeset in Great Britain by
Central Southern Typesetters, Eastbourne
Manufactured in Hong Kong by
Regent Publishing Services Limited
Printed in Hong Kong by
Leefung-Asco Printers Limited

CONTENTS

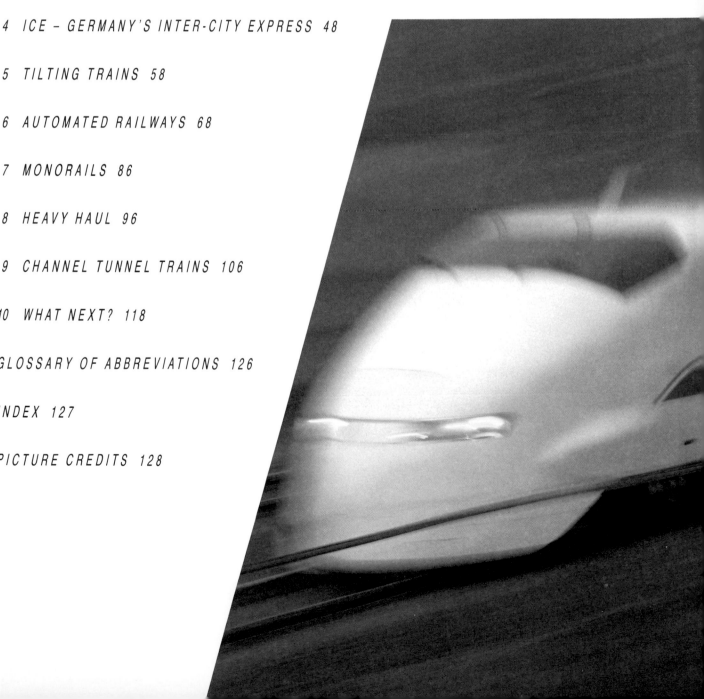

New technology – or "Hi-Tech" – has many applications to modern railways. It is employed at all stages from design and manufacturing to running and maintenance. Probably the greatest hi-tech advance in the past decade has been in the field of electronics. And railways the world over have been quick to make use of advanced electronics in many applications. They include communications, signalling, automation and even traction control. Other advances in machine tools, materials, testing and research have all assisted railways to keep up with – and in many cases to better – their competitors.

DEVELOPMENTS IN THE UNITED STATES

As we shall see in the following chapters, many of the hi-tech developments in railways were pioneered in Europe. This has given the impression that the United States has not employed hi-tech to the same extent. But conditions in North America were different from those in Europe. Not only were all the railroads privately owned, but they were also unable to react to the effects of growing competition. American railroads were "common carriers" – i.e., they were unable, because of statutory regulation, to be selective and could not exploit one market at the expense of another. Passenger services were particularly hard hit by competition from the internal airlines and by private motoring, which enjoyed the benefit of extremely cheap fuel. No services could be withdrawn without the approval of the appropriate regulatory authority. The authorities were notoriously slow-moving and bureau-

cratic, but even so by 1968 American railroads were operating only around 500 long-haul passenger trains a day (compared to 15,000 per day in 1942).

The birth of Amtrak in 1971, a public corporation part-financed by the Federal administration, did little to help. Its commercial freedom was limited, and many railroads found it just as difficult to make profits out of carrying freight. That and the refusal of administrations and unions to change time-worn operating and manning practices hampered any improvement in efficiency.

But progress has been made in the United States, although without the incentive of viable passenger traffic, development has not been so spectacular. In such a large country, the introduction of computers has benefited the railways. For example, what is now known as "TOPS" – Total Operations Processing System – had its origin on the Southern Pacific Railroad. In a system where wagons can so easily be "lost", because of the vast distances they travel, the installation of computers to provide an immediate check on the availability, state of repair and deployment of all vehicles was invaluable.

American railroads were among the first to adopt electrification, but in many cases traffic did not produce a sufficient return on investment for wholesale modernization. An exception was the north-east corridor, where the lines of the former Pennsylvania and New York Central Railroads, later Penn Central, were kept reasonably up to date. Elsewhere, with cheap oil and highly standardized and relatively cheap locomotives, dieselization shows an immediate return on capital and electrification has been abandoned in favour of diesel. Other exceptions are urban transit systems and main lines with a high

traffic density. The lines of the north-east corridor, particularly between New York and Washington DC, carry a relatively heavy (although subsidized) passenger traffic on a modernized line with, in places, speeds up to 200 km/h (125 mph). Politics have also played a major part in the fortunes of American railroads, probably even more so than in Europe.

THIRD WORLD RAILWAYS

Railways in the developing countries look at what is happening in the Western World. There are several countries with fairly advanced electrification systems, e.g. South Africa, India, China, Pakistan and Zimbabwe. In most of them their hi-tech equipment originates in Europe or Japan. Much of the Third World is still operating first-generation diesel locomotives, with fairly simple mechanical technology. Some countries are now building their own locomotives and rolling stock, and this trend will no doubt increase as the countries themselves develop. Computerization of control and signalling systems is now being introduced, but has to remain for the time being in the hands of foreign specialists until enough local people have been trained to operate them.

ORIGINS OF RAILWAYS

Let us have a brief look at how it all began. The first public train, from Liverpool to Manchester in 1830, was an example of early 19th-century high technology. George Stephenson had developed a boiler for his steam locomotive *Rocket*, which was revolutionary in that it embodied a number of small tubes running through it. These provided a large heating surface for the hot gases that passed through them from the firebox to boil the water in the boiler. The tubes were a considerable improvement over the one or two large diameter flues that were previously used. Moreover, after doing work in

the cylinders, the steam was not merely exhausted into the atmosphere. It was led instead into the base of the chimney and, by means of a suitably shaped nozzle, was used to increase the draft on the fire in the firebox. This, in turn, helped to match the production of steam to the demand, within the limit of the size of the fire grate. This principle has been used in steam locomotives, with very few exceptions, ever since.

Technology in the railway industry kept pace with other developments and, with the need for ever shorter journey times, speeds increased and even newer technology was brought in to play. Signalling and braking are notable examples, both being necessary in the interests of safety. As signalling developed and, with the invention of the telegraph, embraced telecommunication, degrees of automation were introduced. Signal engineering became a highly technical business. To meet the need for a high degree of safety, automatic brakes, which failed safe, became a must.

ELECTRIC AND DIESEL TECHNOLOGY

While steam locomotive engineering remained relatively "low-tech", the introduction of electric traction in the early years of the 20th century brought a newer and, for the period, higher technology to the scene. The development of the internal combustion engine into a reliable prime mover also saw another technology introduced into rail traction. In the first two decades of this century several experiments were made with both petrol and oil

LEFT TO RIGHT TGV South-East (France); Series 200 Shinkansen (Japan); XPT (Australia); ICE (Germany); APT-E (Britain).

engines powering locomotives and railcars. Some of these were successful, others disastrous.

Electrical technology offered a number of potential advantages, not least of which was the possibility of pulling heavier loads at much higher speeds. Unlike a steam locomotive, an electric locomotive does not have to carry its fuel with it. It has access to relatively unlimited power from sources remote from the train by means of electrical conductors. High-speed trials with electric traction were made in Germany in 1903 on a 23.3 km (14½ mile) stretch of military railway between Marienfelde and Zossen near Berlin. Two electric railcars reached speeds of around 210 km/h (130 mph), but not without coming dangerously close to derailment in one case because of the limitations of the track and the vehicles themselves.

The potential of electric traction is also attractive in countries where coal is expensive to produce or has to be imported. There is a particular attraction in mountainous countries where electricity can be generated cheaply by means of water power and used to drive the powerful locomotives needed to move heavy trains at reasonable speeds on steep gradients. Lines in the mountainous countries of Europe and the United States are examples of early electric traction schemes used to advantage.

The other major challenge to steam traction did not really materialize until the late 1930s. The early examples of petrol- and diesel-electric railcars in Sweden, Germany and Switzerland pointed the way, but it was in the United States that the internal combustion compression-ignition (diesel) engine really found its mark. With coal available relatively cheaply only in the eastern and southern states, oil was used to fuel some of the larger steam locomotives. But large quantities of water had to be carried when negotiating near-desert terrain. Also the low thermal efficiency of the steam locomotive encouraged the development of diesel locomotives and self-propelled passenger units, in which a given amount of oil consumed produced nearly three times the amount of work. By the late 1940s, there was a real need for a more flexible alternative to the very large and special-purpose steam locomotives required to haul long and heavy freight trains at reasonable speeds, particularly over the long grades of the mountainous regions. That requirement was comfortably met by modestly powered diesel-electric locomotives, which were run in sets of three, four or more under the control of one crew. Moreover additional "helper" locomotives could be spliced into trains at almost any point or at the rear, and so ease the strain on the drawbar of the leading vehicle. Later these helper units were to be remotely controlled by radio from the leading units.

HIGH TECHNOLOGY

It is since the demise of steam traction that really hi-tech systems have been applied to railways. Faced with ever-growing competition from road and air, railways have had to attract their customers by offering something not offered by alternative modes of transport. Most important of these have been cleanliness and comfort, with competitive transit times between city centres. This, in turn, involves very high-speed running on both existing and new tracks. It has also meant installing more power and the development of better permanent way, signalling and train-control systems, and greater refinement of vehicle dynamics.

It was competition from the electric tramcar (street car) that prompted the electrification of urban and sub-urban lines in the early part of this century around large centres of population in Europe and the United States. A multiplicity of different systems emerged, and some of those have subsequently disappeared. Electrification offers much more than most other traction systems, and this is where the major applications of advanced technology are found today. In the rapid transit field, the trend is being reversed and tramways, having been displaced in many places by buses and cars, are now having a revival in the form of so-called Light Rapid Transit

systems. Many of these employ high technology; some even entirely new technology.

So far, very high-speed passenger trains run on conventional tracks and in most cases have conventional suspensions — albeit mainly on new railway lines. For the future it is likely we shall see active suspensions — the tilt mechanism of the ill-fated APT (Advanced Passenger Train) on British Rail was an example of an active suspension; the current Italian system is also active. And by using micro-processors, the detection and control problems are very much reduced.

Electric traction has a great future, and we are at last beginning to see the maintenance man's dream — the almost maintenance-free traction motor. In technical terms it is a three-phase squirrel-cage ac motor, which brings with it the bonus of regenerative braking. With state-of-the-art electronics (the missing link 80 years ago), it is possible to convert direct to alternating current, and to transform a single-phase ac fixed-frequency supply into three-phase variable frequency. There are a number of such types in service already, and valuable experience is being gained in locomotives and self-propelled (multiple-unit) trains on both sides of the Atlantic.

Other guided transport systems will undoubtedly be developed. The most promising so far seems to be Maglev — magnetically-levitated vehicles that "hover" over special tracks. One low-speed system has been operating in Britain for seven years between Birmingham Airport and Birmingham International railway station. Experiments with very high speed Maglev systems are being conducted in Japan and Germany, and much investigatory work has also been done at Pueblo in the United States. So far no one system has been shown to be ahead of its rivals, and all have to perfect methods which give complete integrity of levitation and braking.

It is not only traction systems that are forging ahead. Signalling and telecommunication engineers now have sophisticated train control and train protection systems at their command. High-speed lines like the Japanese

Shinkansen, French TGV and German NBS (*Neubaustrecke*) would not be possible without automatic train protection (ATP). On new lines conventional visual signalling is no longer necessary or desirable, and all of the information needed by the driver can be provided in the form of a visual display in the cab. Train speeds can be regulated without the intervention of the driver and, in an emergency, immediate action can be taken automatically.

The civil and permanent way engineers have not been idle either. Track switches, or points, have been developed for very high speeds. New track-laying and repair techniques are being developed which do away with the lengthy periods of restricted running previously necessary, and, with the aid also of automatic train protection, delays can be cut to a minimum. Much more is known today of the interaction between vehicles and the track, and with the help of track-testing vehicles the state of the permanent way can be analysed frequently and with greater efficiency.

What of the vehicles themselves? Passenger safety is rightly of great concern to vehicle designers. Today much more is known of the behaviour of vehicle structures, while suspensions ensure a smooth and safe ride at all times. Air suspensions are now commonplace, and active suspensions are being introduced. The possibility of combining the two is very attractive.

Freight vehicles are also being transformed and the introduction of inter-modal vehicles, particularly in North America and Australia, is of immense importance.

This is a particularly interesting time for students of railways and many technical developments are taking place. The following chapters give an insight into the key innovations of recent years.

9

TGV –
FRANCE'S TRAINS A GRANDE VITESSE

*T*he French national railway – Société National de Chemin de Fer, or SNCF – has always been conscious of the importance of speed. As soon as possible after World War II it put in hand the electrification of the line from Paris to Lyons and Marseilles, using direct current (dc) at 1500 volts. By 1952 SNCF had an Inter-City service in the 113-121 km/h (70-75 mph) average speed range. But they were not content with that.

ABOVE One of the first new trains for the Paris-Lyon TGV line (TGV – South East) is seen traversing the typical terrain of central France. The spacing between the tracks is greater than used on "normal" lines and helps to reduce buffeting when trains pass.

TESTING TIMES

The start of the 1950s saw SNCF embarking on a continuous research programme designed to test the speed potential of orthodox steel wheels on steel rails. By June 1954, one of their newest Co-Co electric locomotives achieved a speed of 225 km/h (140 mph) on the Paris-Lyons line near Beaune. A later test with a pair of Co-Co electric locomotives hauling a 610-tonne (600-ton) train revealed that much research was needed into the problem of maintaining consistently good current collection at high speeds. It took the best part of two decades to solve the problem.

In the spring of 1955, further tests at much higher speeds were made on the older 1500V dc line running from Paris to the Spanish border. Two locomotives hauling lightweight trains both achieved a speed of 330.9 km/h (205.6 mph) south of Bordeaux on modified stan-

LEFT An impression of one of the new TGV-A trains at speed. Note, in comparison to the TGV-E, improvements made to the aerodynamic form.

dard track and under catenaries which were of 1927 technology. While these speeds remained unbeaten for the next 26 years, the current collection problems were so severe that collectors disintegrated. The track was also severely distorted and it was clear that to achieve speeds much higher than the then normal 145-160 km/h (90-100 mph) much work was needed on locomotive and vehicle dynamics, and on track technology. On the other hand, a speed of 320 km/h (200 mph) looked as though it should be attainable.

By the end of the 1950s, competition from Air Inter – France's internal air service – was threatening to erode SNCF's inter-city traffic and it was essential to reduce travelling times between cities. By 1961 a speed of 200 km/h (125 mph) had been authorized for two Capitol trains over 50 km (31.1 miles) of the Paris-Toulouse line between St Aubrais (Orléans) and Vierzon. Here for the first time hi-tech cab signalling and automatic train control apparatus were used. A second phase of 200 km/h (125 mph) was inaugurated, but this time new rolling stock with advanced suspensions was introduced. These vehicles, known as "Grand Confort" cars, were designed to incorporate body-tilting which was to have been fitted at a later stage.

Experience showed that the speeds did not warrant sophisticated and complicated automatic train control, and this was abandoned in favour of a change in the signalling to give advanced warning of a possible signal stop ahead. This minimized the cost of preparing two-thirds of the Paris-Bordeaux main line for 200 km/h (125 mph) running. By 1971 one trip in each direction daily was timed at an average speed of 151 km/h (93.8 mph), using conventional locomotives and rolling stock.

THE BIRTH OF TGV

In October 1964, the Japanese launched the Shinkansen (New Railway) between Tokyo and Osaka, a distance of 515 km (320 miles) at a time when railways were struggling to establish 160 km/h (100 mph) as a standard for express trains between large centres of population (see Chapter 2). This event fired determination on both sides of the Atlantic for higher rail speeds, and in the summer of 1964 SNCF initiated a study of a similar high-speed railway between Paris and France's second city, Lyons. This route was the main artery of French social and commercial life, and the main route to most of southern and south-eastern France. The existing route had a serious bottleneck in the Burgundy hills to the north of Dijon, which was also the junction for the capital's main access to southern Switzerland and Italy.

The old PLM (Paris-Lyons-Mediterranean Railway) main line was saturated and the cost of increasing its capacity by quadrupling would not be value for money because of speed constraints on the winding route. For these reasons, a new special-purpose high-speed line for passenger trains only was proposed. This line would cross central France's vast tracts of open country and could easily be made environmentally-friendly. The new-found technology would reduce its capital cost to a fraction of that of the Japanese Shinkansen. It took a further 10 years of planning, research and development, not to mention countering opposition from ecological and road transport interests intent on thwarting the project, before construction began with the blessing of the French Government in December 1976. This was the start of the first Ligne à Grand Vitesse (LGV).

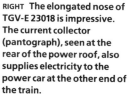

RIGHT **The elongated nose of TGV-E 23018 is impressive. The current collector (pantograph), seen at the rear of the power roof, also supplies electricity to the power car at the other end of the train.**

ABOVE **Inside the maintenance depot, special cradles are supporting a trailer car while work is being carried out. The** adjacent ends of two vehicles share one bogie; such special arrangements must be made when changing bogies.

LINES OF THE TGV-SE

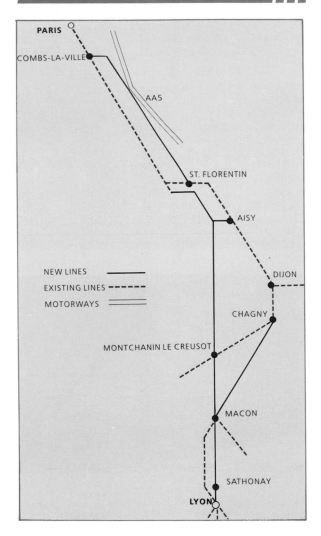

Some of the enormous cost of building a new line was avoided by using the existing main line for the first 29.9 km (18.6 miles) from Paris Gare de Lyon and rejoining it on the outskirts of Lyons. Between these points the engineering was similar to that of a motorway, but of much reduced width – it actually shares the infrastructure with two autoroutes (motorways) for a total of 71 km (44 miles). To minimize expensive earthworks, the LGV hugs the contours with gradients as steep as 1 in 28.5 (3.5 per cent), close to the usual autoroute limit of 1 in 25 (4 per cent), with curvature only slightly more generous than the autoroute norm.

TGV trains do not employ any body-tilting mechanism but with exclusive use of the route by standard trains, the curves can be safely negotiated even at 257-270 km/h (160-170 mph). This is because the track has the ideal cant and because of the design of the low centre-of-gravity, lightweight vehicles and suspension. Additionally, by sticking close to the contours, there was no need for any tunnels along the 390 km (242 miles) of new line.

The new line is very simple. There are only two intermediate stations, at Le Creusot (Montchanin) and Macon, with three junctions in addition to those at each end. One junction feeds some TGV trains to Dijon, Switzerland and the French Alps. In addition, because TGVs are compatible with the existing system, they run beyond the limits of the new line to Montpellier, Marseilles and beyond. Since not all trains stop at the new intermediate stations, the two platforms at each are served by loops which, like the junctions with the old line, are designed to be taken at up to 220 km/h (137 mph). In addition, emergency crossovers are installed at regular intervals and sidings are provided at a number of places to hold failed trains. Even so, the number of switches is minimal.

13

THE TRAINS

Experience in the 1960s with gas turbine powered "Turbotrains" culminated in the reasonably successful lightweight RTG sets. Power requirements for TGV would be high, and the only prime mover that could reasonably be employed was a version of the lightweight aircraft-type gas turbine similar to those used in the RTG sets. A five-car articulated gas turbine-electric prototype train was built in 1972. During a programme of prolonged trials, some 54,716 km (34,000 miles) were run at more than 200 km/h (125 mph) in the six years to the train's retirement in 1978. By 1974, however, the oil price explosion had rendered gas turbine propulsion uneconomic, and SNCF had no option but to electrify.

One operational advantage of gas turbine propulsion was the ability to run into non-electrified territory (for example, from Lyons to Grenoble) or to use lines electrified on different systems. But now it became economic even to electrify those routes. The system chosen for TGV was single-phase ac at 25kV and a frequency of 50Hz, but as this was not compatible with the former PLM lines, electrified at 1500V dc, the new trains would have to incur the weight penalty of having both systems. This would also give access to Marseilles and Geneva, but any extension to operation over the lines of the Swiss Federal Railways would require three-system equipment to allow operation over their lines that use 15kV ac single-phase at 16.6Hz. In the event only a handful of train sets (eight) were built with equipment to enable them to run additionally on the 15kV ac single-phase system.

REDUCING WEIGHT

To minimize weight it was decided to keep the prototype arrangement of articulation for the passenger-carrying vehicles, and the final design was an eight-car articulated unit with a two-bogie Bo-Bo power car at each end — ten vehicles in all with a tare (unladen) weight of 386 tonnes (380 tons). To propel this weight of train over a line with gradients as steep as 1 in 28.5 at the required average speed demands a high output from the traction motors. Accordingly, each power car carries four 525kW (720hp) dc traction motors and additionally feeds two further motors driving the wheels of the leading bogie of the adjacent passenger car, known as a "semi-motrice".

The earlier tests showed that in order to limit the forces between vehicle and track it was necessary to minimize the total weight of the motor-bogies. Instead of the traction motors being carried in the usual way in the bogies themselves, each motor is suspended from the underside of the vehicle and drives its corresponding axle through a short Cardan-type shaft and a gearbox mounted on the bogie frame.

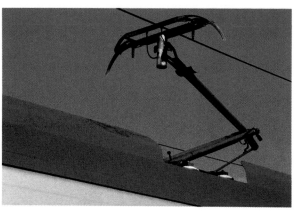

TOP This photograph illustrates an intermediate bogie carrying the ends of two cars. To ensure a good comfortable ride, both vertical and horizontal hydraulic dampers are provided. Damping is also incorporated between the two vehicle ends.

ABOVE The current collector (pantograph) on the TGV-A power car must be sufficiently lightweight to follow the contact wire at the highest speeds. Current is collected by special carbon strips.

CURRENT COLLECTION

There are two pantographs, one for ac operation and one for dc. With normal operation from the 25kV line, current is fed through one pantograph specially designed for the high speeds involved. The leading power car is fed direct, while a roof-mounted 25kV line feeds the rear power car, the connection between each vehicle being made by an inductive link. When two TGV sets are coupled together, as with most trains between Paris and Lyons, the second set is also fed by one of its own pantographs, usually that on the leading power car. For oper-

occurs. Special high-speed lightweight pantographs were designed and tested on existing lines at speeds well in excess of 200 km/h (125 mph) to ensure that current collection was satisfactory.

The first series of trains, now known as TGV-E, have traction equipment with well-known thyristor control, in which the alternating current supply is regulated and rectified to supply dc traction motors. As mentioned earlier, all trains are able to accept alternating current at 25kV and 50Hz or direct current at 1500V. Those required to run over the Swiss Federal Railways to Lausanne also have to accept single-phase alternating current at 15kV and 16.6Hz using the same transformers as for 25kV/50Hz, but at a cost of reduced power to the traction motors. This is unimportant because speeds over the CFF/SBB (Swiss Federal Railways) are limited to 140 km/h.

ABOVE **This photograph shows the secondary air-springs being lowered into position. Note also the three brake discs on the nearest axle. Bogie frames must be rigid but light and great care taken in the design and manufacture. Regular inspections are made during service.**

ation on 1500V dc, the alternative pantographs on both power cars are used.

One of the many lessons learned from high-speed operation has been the importance of matching the performance of pantographs and the overhead system to obtain optimum performance. This must take into account the overhead line dynamics, and the need to prevent a second pantograph being affected by the disturbance in the catenary caused by the passage of the leading pantograph. The higher the speed, the more important it is that continuous contact is maintained or serious arcing

TGV-E (Sud-Est) 23000 SERIES (France)	
GAUGE:	Standard (4 ft 8½ in)
Electrical system:	25kV ac 50hz and 1500V dc
FORMATION:	2+10
Power cars:	2
Semi-motor cars:	2
Trailers:	6
BUILT:	1978–86
Builder:	Alsthom/Francorail-MTE/de Dietrich
Number built:	109
WEIGHTS:	Complete unit: 385 tonnes (378 tons)
Power car:	65 tonnes (63.8 tons)
Semi-motor car:	43 or 44 tonnes (42.2 or 43.2 tons)
Articulated trailer:	28 tonnes (27.5 tons)
DIMENSIONS:	200 m (658 ft 8 in) over couplers
Power car:	22150 mm (72 ft 8 in)
Semi-motor car:	21845 mm (71 ft 8 in)
Articulated trailer:	18700 mm (61 ft 4 in)
SEATING:	111 First, 275 Second
First only sets (9):	287
POWER EQUIPMENT:	Thyristor/Chopper
System:	ac/dc & dc/dc
TRACTION MOTORS:	12×525 kW – total: 6300 kW
Power car:	4
Semi-motor car:	2
MAX PERMITTED SPEED:	280 km/hr (174 mph)
Normal service speed:	270 km/hr (168 mph)
BRAKING SYSTEM:	Electropneumatic and rheostatic
Type:	Disc and tread brakes

TOP As well as providing refreshments and stylish dining accommodation, the buffet car of the TGV-A features a visual display unit, providing information about connecting train times and so on.

ABOVE Inside the cab of an early TGV-A train set, the driver sits to the left of centre. Immediately in front of him is the control for power and normal braking. The various instruments and displays give him a continuous picture of the running conditions.

Using the experience gained with the TGV-E, the new trains for the TGV-Atlantique have been changed in a number of important respects. Each set has two additional cars, giving a 2+10 formation. The original TGV power car bogies have been exceptionally successful and have been retained. The increased speed potential has been made possible because of developments in traction, aerodynamics, braking and current collection. The TGV-A sets have eight ac traction motors of the self-commutating synchronous type, each with a continuous rating of 1100kW. This has been made possible by developments in electronics, to the microprocessor in particular. Traction equipment is confined to the power cars, the weight of which is slightly lower than TGV-E at 67.8 tonnes (66.6 tons).

The bodies of the power cars have been redesigned, with improved aerodynamic styling and a different driver's cab layout. Weight has been saved by using some parts

ABOVE One of the new trains provided for TGV-A. The styling is less "angular" than that of the earlier series, and there are 10 intermediate cars between the two power cars. These trains, like their earlier counterparts, work over existing and new lines and collect current at 1500V dc as well as 25,000V ac.

made from aluminium or a different type of steel. Both traction and auxiliary equipment make use of the latest traction technology, such as freon-cooling, gate turn-off thyristors (GTOs), microprocessor control, electric braking, multiplexing of remote control functions, and so on.

The increased maximum speed has resulted in an improvement in braking performance. It was necessary to eliminate tread brakes to reduce maintenance cost and noise. New high-performance disc brakes have been developed, which increase the brake force by 70 per cent compared to TGV-E. This has been made possible by redesigning the discs and by the use of a microprocessor-controlled system. This latter enables the train to make full use of the available adhesion. In addition, the ac synchronous motors allow the use of a powerful electric brake independent of the power supply.

The interior design of the TGV-A incorporates a number of improvements over its predecessors. There is luxurious

semi-compartment seating in first class, and second class now has fabric-covered seats and window curtains. There are two areas of seating bays which families can use, an area where young children can play, a nursery, special accommodation for the disabled, a new design of bar car and telephones. Each set has seating for 485 passengers as well as 37 fold-down seats for use in peak periods.

The speed capability was amply demonstrated on 23 September 1986, when set No. 10 attained a speed of 356 km/h (221.25 mph) on a publicity run on the LGV-E. This was of course not as high as the record made by one of the original trains in February 1981, when a speed of 380 km/h (236.2 mph) was attained. Subsequently a world record speed of 515.3 km/h (320.19 mph) was achieved near Vendôme on 18 May 1990.

Cab signalling was provided on TGV-E, and while this has been very effective, not to say essential, the system has been up-dated for TGV-A. Extra track circuit codes

TGV-A (Atlantique) 24000 SERIES (France)	
GAUGE:	Standard (4 ft 8 in)
Electrical system:	25kV ac 50hz, 1500V dc
FORMATION:	2+10
Power cars:	2
Trailers:	10
BUILT:	1988–91
Builder:	Alsthom/de Dietrich
Number built:	97
WEIGHTS:	Complete unit: 444 tonnes (436 tons)
Power car:	67.8 tonnes (66.6 tons)
Trailer:	30.8 tonnes (30.24 tons)
DIMENSIONS:	240 m (789 ft 6 in) over couplers
Power car:	22150 mm (72 ft 6½ in)
Trailer car:	18700 mm (61 ft 4 in)
SEATING:	485
First class:	116
Second class:	369
POWER EQUIPMENT:	Synchronous, bi-current
Systems:	ac-dc-3ph ac, dc-3ph ac
TRACTION MOTORS:	8×1100kW – total 8800kW
Power car:	4 each
MAX PERMITTED SPEED:	300 km/hr (186 mph)
Normal service speed:	300 km/hr (186 mph)
BRAKING SYSTEM:	Electropneumatic and regenerative
Type:	Disc and electromagnetic

for the higher speed are necessary. Over the section near Tours, which is used by "conventional" locomotive-hauled trains travelling at 160 or 200 km/h (100-125 mph), special cab displays are provided to supplement the conventional lineside signalling. Gradients on TGV-A line are less severe than TGV-E, 2.5% (1 in 40) against 3.5% (1 in 28.5) and this simplifies the signalling. Braking distances, and hence block sections, can be more or less standardized.

Of particular interest on both types of train is the electronic device fitted to the power cars which continuously monitors the line profile. When it senses a change, it adjusts the power input to the traction motors as required to maintain the speed set by the driver.

USES OF COMPUTERS

Microprocessors have a number of uses, and these are not confined to the traction control system. There are numerous procedures which are now automated which previously were done rather laboriously by hand. Practically all of the pre-departure checking (cab signalling, braking, and so on) is now done automatically. Real-time information can be provided for the driver and on-board train staff about the status of equipment. Correcting problems is easier because fault diagnosis is carried out automatically. Faults can be recorded and the conditions under which they occurred can be sent by radio to the maintenance depot while the train is moving, and many preparations can be initiated by remote radio control.

On all TGV lines a fare supplement, which includes the cost of reserving a seat, is charged. Seat reservation is recorded on a computer, and if a seat is occupied for only part of a journey, for example from Lyons to Le Creusot, it is then made available for another passenger boarding at Le Creusot to travel to Paris.

18

NEW HIGH-SPEED LINES

Following the success of TGV-E, plans were announced for more lines. The first would run from Paris Montparnasse to Le Mans and Tours, taking TGVs to Rennes and Brest in Brittany and Bordeaux. These would be the world's first new lines built to carry trains at 300 km/h (186.5 mph) from the start. The French Government agreed to pay for 30 per

ROUTE OF THE TGV-A

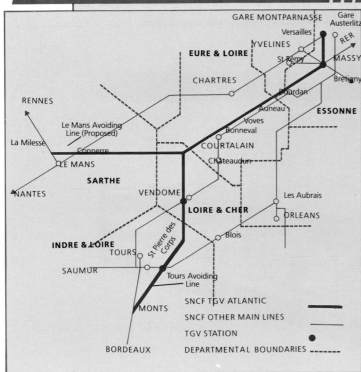

GARE MONTPARNASSE
Gare Austerlitz
Versailles
YVELINES
EURE & LOIRE
St Rémy
MASSY
RER
CHARTRES
Bretigny
Dourdan
RENNES
Auneau
Voves
ESSONNE
Le Mans Avoiding
Line (Proposed)
Bonneval
La Milesse
Connerre
COURTALAIN
LE MANS
Châteaudun
SARTHE
VENDOME
Les Aubrais
NANTES
LOIRE & CHER
ORLEANS
St Pierre des Corps
Blois
INDRE & LOIRE
TOURS
SAUMUR
Tours Avoiding Line
MONTS
SNCF TGV ATLANTIC
SNCF OTHER MAIN LINES
TGV STATION
BORDEAUX
DEPARTMENTAL BOUNDARIES

OPPOSITE A TGV-A train passes over the rooftops along the viaduct at Morlaix in Brittany.

ABOVE The overhead gear of the TGV has been specially developed so that the pantographs can feed a continuous current to the power car. At high speeds, serious arcing occurs when contact is not maintained.

cent of the civil engineering costs of the new line, which has many tunnels and viaducts. Also in the southern suburbs of Paris, between Massy-Palaiseau and Chatillon, the line adopted the never-completed line from Paris to Chartres via Gallardon. The gradients on the TGV-Atlantique are a great deal easier than on the Lyons line, but there are more tunnels, some of them artificial – that is, the line has been deliberately buried for environmental reasons.

At Courtalain, 130 km (80.8 miles) from Paris, the line splits and the 87-km (54-mile) southern arm runs first to Vendôme, the only

intermediate station. Trains for the Tours line can run through the junction at full speed. Extensive tests were made through switches at 320 km/h (199 mph) on the TGV Sud-Est line before setting this standard. Trains for the Le Mans line are restricted to 220 km/h (136.7 mph). Not all trains stop at Tours, so a bypass line was built round the south of the city. It is not exclusive to TGVs because part of the old main line was saturated, and special signalling arrangements have been made.

Like the other TGV lines, electrification is at 25kV ac single-phase except for the two ends and the Tours bypass, which use the existing 1500V dc system. TGVs are limited to 220 km/h (136.7 mph) over the old lines between Tours and Bordeaux.

19

There are two different approaches to the use of three-phase ac traction motors. The Germans and Swiss (Brown Boveri Ltd) favoured and developed the three-phase asynchronous type of motor, which has no electrical connection between the stator (frame) and the rotor. This is known as the squirrel cage motor because of the configuration of the winding on the rotor. SNCF favoured the synchronous type that has a wound rotor fed through slip rings because the control circuitry is somewhat less complex.

It is this latter type which, following successful trials in an experimental set-up in a converted locomotive, has been adopted for TGV-A. The technique was first intended as the future standard SNCF practice for main-line motive power, including the 190 TGV-A power cars and 44 Sybic (Synchronous B-current) locomotives. It seems that there were many teething problems and it is now clear that the system will not be the future standard. Asynchronous traction motors will be used on the joint SNCF-BR-SNCB Channel Tunnel through trains.

EQUIPMENT LAYOUT OF THE TGV-A POWER CAR

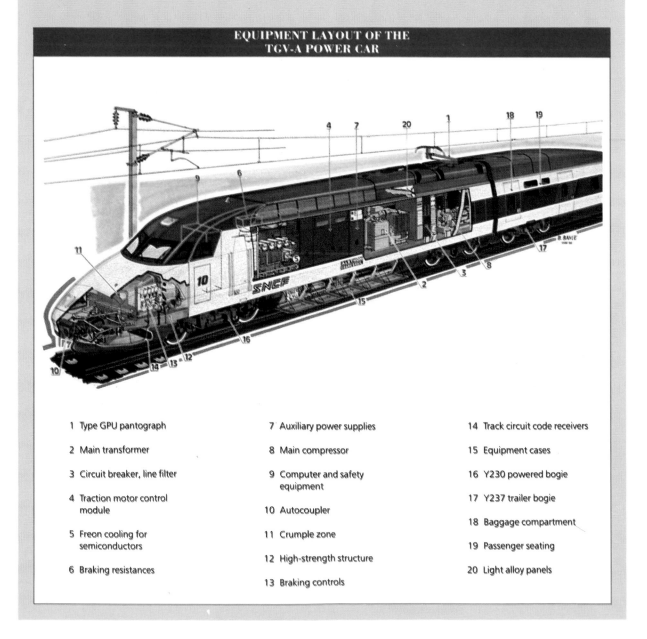

1 Type GPU pantograph	7 Auxiliary power supplies	14 Track circuit code receivers
2 Main transformer	8 Main compressor	15 Equipment cases
3 Circuit breaker, line filter	9 Computer and safety equipment	16 Y230 powered bogie
4 Traction motor control module	10 Autocoupler	17 Y237 trailer bogie
5 Freon cooling for semiconductors	11 Crumple zone	18 Baggage compartment
6 Braking resistances	12 High-strength structure	19 Passenger seating
	13 Braking controls	20 Light alloy panels

20

TGV AND THE CHANNEL TUNNEL

Even before the advent of the Channel Tunnel, SNCF was considering a new TGV line from Paris to Lille. This would also form the first part of a high-speed route linking Paris with Brussels, Cologne and Amsterdam. With a Channel Tunnel there would be sufficient traffic to justify such a line. The new line, TGV-Nord, is now materialising and, unlike on the British side, will convey the very high-speed cross-channel trains to the French tunnel portal.

These new trains, the Trans Manche Super Trains (TMSTs) – discussed in detail in chapter 9 – have been developed from the TGVs by GEC-Alsthom. Major modifications were necessary so that the trains could suit the diverse requirements of the Belgian, French and British networks. In the area of current collection alone, British Rail has a 750V dc third-rail system, the Belgians a 3000V dc overhead system, SNCF a 1500V dc overhead system and, of course, the Channel Tunnel itself employs a 25kV ac 50Hz system. So compatibility was a key consideration.

BELOW In this prototype of the Channel Tunnel system, the two outer running tunnels can be clearly seen on either side of the service tunnel. A Channel Tunnel shuttle train emerges on the left, while a service vehicle disappears on the right.

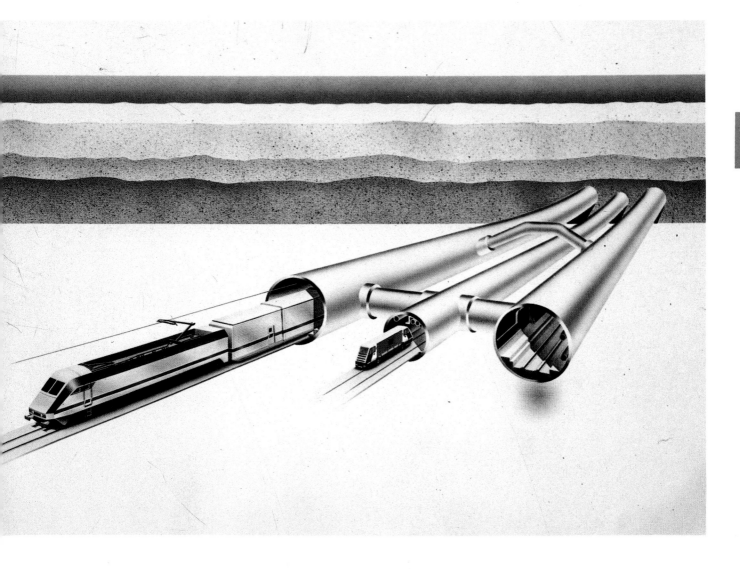

21

SHINKANSEN

THE JAPANESE "BULLET" TRAINS

OPPOSITE **The Shinkansen trains travel through densely populated urban areas, so environ mental considerations at present dictate a top speed of 270 km/h (168 mph) – even though they are capable of much higher speeds.**

Since 1939, the world record for the highest scheduled speeds had been held by the Italian Railways. To bolster Mussolini's claim of Italy's technical supremacy on land, a special demonstration run was staged between Florence and Milan over the Direttissima on 20 July 1939. A three-car articulated set ran the 315.1 km (195.8 miles) at an average speed of 164.2 km/h (102 mph), with a maximum speed of 202.8 km/h (126 mph). This was to remain unbeaten until the completion of the Japanese Shinkansen (New Railway), the Tokaido line, in 1960.

THE BIRTH OF SHINKANSEN

The post-World War II population and industrial explosion in the coastal belt between Tokyo and Osaka forced the Japanese National Railways (JNR) to find a way to expand operating capacity. JNR and the government concluded it was futile to even try to find the extra capacity from the existing 3 ft 6 in gauge Tokaido main line, which in any event was too restricted by frequent level crossings – a thousand of them – and almost continuously lined by buildings. Since it was almost entirely passenger traffic that was expanding at an alarming rate, and due to the inherent constraints of the narrow-gauge system, it was decided to build an entirely new standard gauge

ABOVE **Mount Fujiyama towers over a 100N Series "bullet" train moving at speed.**

SHINKANSEN 100 Series (Japan)	
ELECTRICAL SYSTEM:	AC25kV – 60 Hz
CONFIGURATION:	12M4T
NOMINAL RIDING CAPACITY:	Second class – 1153 First class – 168
WEIGHT:	Train set – 925
MAXIMUM SPEED: Balancing speed on level line: Starting acceleration:	220 km/h (132 mph) 276 km/h (171 mph) 1.60 km/h/s (.96 mph/s)
POWER RUNNING CONTROL SYSTEM:	Thryistor continuous phase control
BRAKE CONTROL SYSTEM:	Rheostatic brake system and electrically-controlled air brake system (T cars equipped with eddy current brake system ECB) Continuous control along adhesion pattern
BODY CONSTRUCTION:	Made of steel; equipment underslung and interspersed with dummy plates

BODY DIMENSIONS
Lead car –
   length:
   width:
   height:
Intermediate car –
   length:
   width:
   height:
Double-decker car –
   length:
   width:
   height:
	
	25.80 m (84 ft 7½ in)
	3.38 m (11 ft 1½ in)
	4.00 m (13 ft 1½ in)
	
	24.50 m (80 ft 4½ in)
	3.38 m (11 ft 1½ in)
	4.00 m (13 ft 1½ in)
	
	24.50m (80 ft 4½ in)
	3.38 m (11 ft 1½ in)
	4.49 m (14 ft 9 in)

BOGIE: Wheel diameter: Wheel base:	Bolster type, end beams 0.91m (3 ft 0 in) 2.50m (8 ft 2½ in)
TRACTION MOTOR:	DC series-wound motor MT 202 48 motors/train set 230 kW/motor Forced ventilation system 11040 kW/train set
GEAR RATIO:	1:2:41 (27:65)
AUXILIARY POWER SOURCE:	Stationary voltage stabilizer AC-DC 100V Auxiliary transformer AC 100V Tertiary winding AC 400V
PANTOGRAPH:	PS 202 (sensitive contact strip) 5 pantographs/train set (preparation for reduction by half)
ATC:	Single-frequency system (preparation for double-frequency system)

(1435 mm, or 4 ft 8½ in) railway from Tokyo to Osaka, which would also cater for important towns and cities in between. The existing narrow-gauge line would be left to handle freight and any intermediate passenger business.

The new railway would be designed to cater for a quantum leap in speed and comfort and, because it was being built for a single purpose, it could be engineered for one type of train only. The new line would be electrified on the 25kV ac single-phase 60Hz system, and the trains would be fixed-formation, high power/weight ratio multiple units capable of travelling at a normal maximum speed of 210 km/h (130 mph). It was envisaged that there would be a very frequent service of trains from dawn to dusk, day in and day out. Trains would be standard, running at standard speeds over a double-track line and supervised from one control centre in Tokyo. The network would be comparatively uncomplicated – with only 230 sets of points (switches), including the depots, on the whole route. It was comparatively easy to devise an automatic train control system which would give the driver a multi-aspect signalling display in his cab. This system would be activated by coded impulses in the running rails, with decoding apparatus on the trains themselves. The New Tokaido Line would be the first ever trunk route to dispense with trackside signalling. Construction of the New Railway commenced in 1959.

THE TRAINS

The new trains were formed of multiples of 2-car units, and the maximum could be eight 2-car units to form a 16-car train. The front and rear cars were similar except that only one carried a pantograph. The streamlining incorporated a nose cone, so that they immediately became known as "bullet" trains. The gross weight of a 16-car train totalled 880 tonnes (866 tons), and there were seats for up to 1300 people, depending on the proportion of first- to second-class accommodation. Every axle of every car was driven by a bogie-mounted dc traction motor with a continuous rating of 185kW (248hp) – equivalent to 11,840kW (15,875hp) for a 16-car train – and a pantograph current collector was provided on one car of each 2-car unit. The pantograph car carried a 1650kVA transformer and a 1627kW silicon rectifier to supply eight traction motors (both cars) and the associated control gear. The design maximum speed was 210 km/h (130 mph). Details of the various cars which form the trains are given in the table.

In 1963, 1022 Shinkansen cars were delivered, with enough driving cars to form 109 trains. A further 450 non-driving cars were delivered in 1964, 57 more in 1966, and a final batch of 139 in 1969 – a grand total of 1668 cars. Particular care was taken to reduce drag and all cars

SHINKANSEN 200 Series (Japan)	
ELECTRICAL SYSTEM:	AC25kV – 60 Hz
CONFIGURATION:	16M
NOMINAL RIDING CAPACITY:	Second class – 1208 First class – 132
WEIGHT:	Train set – 970
MAXIMUM SPEED: Balancing speed on level line: Starting acceleration:	220 km/h (132 mph) 235 km/h (141 mph) 1.00 km/h/s (.6 mph/s)
POWER RUNNING CONTROL SYSTEM:	Low-voltage tap switching step control
BRAKE CONTROL SYSTEM:	Rheostatic brake system and electromagnetic straight air brake system Control according to ATC speed step
BODY CONSTRUCTION:	Made of steel; equipment underslung

BODY DIMENSIONS
Lead car –
  length:
  width:
  height:
Intermediate car –
  length:
  width:
  height:
	
	24.90 m (81 ft 8½ in)
	3.38 m (11 ft 1½ in)
	3.975 m (13 ft ½ in)
	
	24.50 m (80 ft 4½ in)
	3.38 m (11 ft ½ in)
	3.975 m (13 ft ½ in)

BOGIE: Wheel diameter: Wheel base:	Bolster type, with end beams 0.91m (3 ft 0 in) 2.50m (8 ft 2½ in)
TRACTION MOTOR:	DC series-wound motor MT 200B 64 motors/train set 185 kW/motor Self-ventilation system 11840 kW/train set
GEAR RATIO:	1:2:17 (29:69)
AUXILIARY POWER SOURCE:	Rotary motor generator AC-DC 100V Auxiliary rectifier DC 100V Auxiliary transformer AC 100V Tertiary winding AC 220V
PANTOGRAPH:	PS 200 8 pantographs/train set
ATC:	Single-frequency system

SHINKANSEN 300 Series (Japan)	
ELECTRICAL SYSTEM:	AC25kV – 60 Hz
CONFIGURATION:	10MGT
NOMINAL RIDING CAPACITY:	Second class – 1123 First class – 200
WEIGHT:	Train set – 710
MAXIMUM SPEED: Balancing speed on level line: Starting acceleration:	270 km/h (162 mph) 296 km/h (177 mph) 1.60 km/h/s (.96 mph/s)
POWER RUNNING CONTROL SYSTEM:	VVVF (variable voltage variable frequency) control
BRAKE CONTROL SYSTEM:	AC regenerative brake system and electrically-controlled air brake system (T cars equipped with eddy current brake system with load response device Continuous control along adhesion pattern
BODY CONSTRUCTION:	Made of aluminium alloy, equipment underslung and interspersed with dummy plates

BODY DIMENSIONS
Lead car –
  length:
  width:
  height:
Intermediate car –
  length:
  width:
  height:
	
	25.80 m (84 ft 7½ in)
	3.38 m (11 ft 1½ in)
	3.60 m (11 ft 9½ in)
	
	24.50 m (80 ft 4½ in)
	3.38 m (11 ft 1½ in)
	3.60 m (11 ft 9½ in)

BOGIE: Wheel diameter: Wheel base:	Bolsterless type, no end beams 0.86m (2 ft 10 in) 2.50m (8 ft 2½ in)
TRACTION MOTOR:	3-phase cage asynchronous motor TMT1 (TMT2) 40 motors/train set Forced ventilation system 12000 kW/train set
GEAR RATIO:	1:2:96 (23:68)
AUXILIARY POWER SOURCE:	Stationary voltage stabilizer AC-DC 100V Auxiliary transformer AC 100V Tertiary winding AC 400V
PANTOGRAPH:	TPS 203 (double-factor suspended system) 2 pantographs/train set (planned)
ATC:	Double-frequency system

25

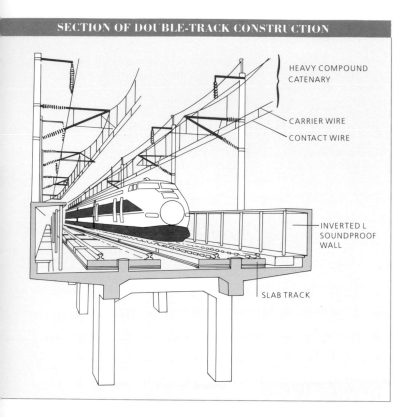

SECTION OF DOUBLE-TRACK CONSTRUCTION

HEAVY COMPOUND CATENARY

CARRIER WIRE

CONTACT WIRE

INVERTED L SOUNDPROOF WALL

SLAB TRACK

had a smooth exterior with most of the under-car equipment behind farings. After a life of some 20 years, the original rolling stock was replaced. The replacements look very much like the originals, but incorporate improvements based on running experience.

French high-speed trials in 1954 and 1955 had shown up special problems with overhead current collection at high speeds. The Japanese, in order to reduce both wind resistance and inertia, designed and installed specially small pantographs. The driving motor car at one end of each train (type 21) has no control gear or pantograph, the motors being fed from the adjacent non-driving motor car.

THE ROUTE

An entirely new route was chosen, although it does run roughly parallel to the original narrow-gauge line for much of the distance. It was chosen to connect the principal towns, but the total number of stations on the new line was limited to 12, including the two terminals. Each intermediate station has a standardized design of two island platforms. One of these is as far as possible straight, so that a stopping train can be held in the "loop" and be overtaken by a fast train where and when required.

LEFT The 200 Series Shinkansen, here running on the East Japan Railway, incorporates several high-tech features, including powerful motors allowing speeds of 275km/h (172mph) anti-snow and anti-cold features and the highly efficient continuous braking system.

THE SERVICE

The new Tokaido line was inaugurated for limited traffic on 1 October 1964, and the full service commenced just two years later. There were two types of train. The Kodama express called at each intermediate station and covered the 515 km (320 miles) in four hours, an average speed of 128 km/h (80 mph). The Hikari super-express called at two intermediate stations and took 3 hours 10 minutes, at an average speed of 162.6 km/h (101 mph).

In spite of the very high construction and operating costs, the success of the new line was demonstrated by a healthy surplus revenue over and above the capital and depreciation charges and running costs. This occurred in spite of the absurdly low fares that the Japanese Government imposed on the JNR.

So popular was the new line that it was decided to push on to Hakata in Kodama Island, the extension being known as the New Sanyo line. This gave a continuous high-speed line 1069 km (664 miles) long. In 1970, the Japanese Government was so enthusiastic that it called for no fewer than six more Shinkansen, which were intended to be just the first instalment of a network of 18 new lines totalling around 7000 km (4350 miles) to promote industrial development and population dispersal

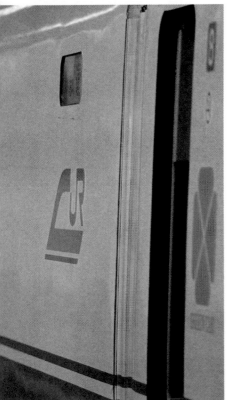

LEFT The smart uniforms worn by Shinkansen train crews serve to emphasize the importance to the network of good customer relations.

away from the already overcrowded coastal belts. In the event only two more Shinkansen have been built so far. The Tohoku Shinkansen runs 500 km (310 miles) from Tokyo to Morioka, with plans to extend it to Sapporo on Hokkaido Island via the Seikan Tunnel. The Joetsu Shinkansen runs from Tokyo to Niigata, while the original Tokaido Shinkansen is being extended towards Kagoshima adding another 435 km (270 miles), or 1500 km (935 miles) in all.

Work on the new lines began in 1971 and they were to have been completed by 1976. But progress was slow because of strong and consistent – sometimes militant – opposition from residents and other groups, often on environmental grounds. This pushed up the costs, and the Joetsu line ran into problems when unexpected unstable rock formations were found during boring of the Nakayama Tunnel between Takasaki and Jomokogen. Limited passenger working was inaugurated on the Tohoku line on 23 June 1982, with a full daily service on 15 November 1982. On the same date a full high-speed service was introduced on the Joetsu line, with 11 fast Morning Sun (Ashai) trains in each direction.

BELOW The Tohuku and Joetsu Shinkansen travel through some of Japan's heaviest snowfall regions. As well as the snowproof, cold-resistant car bodies other features can be found at track-side: automatic snow-removing sprinklers, electric hot-air snow-melting devices (which remove snow near points) and hot water jets.

COPING WITH NATURE

28

In addition to the well-known operating hazards found in Britain and elsewhere in Europe, Japan has to contend also with typhoons and earthquakes. The Control Centre has indicators for wind speeds and earth tremors and, for the Tohoku line in particular, two groups of sensors to detect any significant movements on the sea bed. This data allows the Control Centre to decide whether to reduce train speeds – in extreme conditions it may be necessary to suspend the train service altogether.

Special arrangements have also to be made to contend with exceptionally heavy snowfalls where the lines pass through the trans-Alpine region. There falls of 3 m or more are not exceptional, and an elaborate water-sprinkling, snow-warming system has been developed. On the Joetsu line it is used over a total of 76 km (47 miles). Elsewhere snow is cleared from the tracks by the snowplough which forms an integral part of the nose-structure of the 200 Series trains used on those lines.

THE SHINKANSEN NETWORK

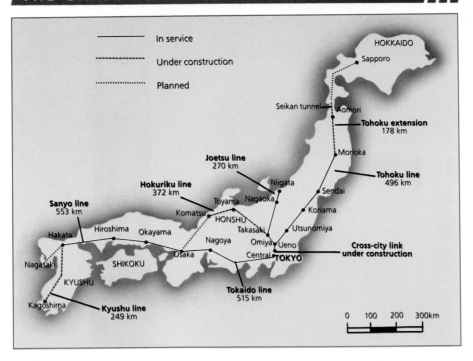

HOKKAIDO
- Sapporo

— In service

---- Under construction

········ Planned

Seikan tunnel · Aomori

Tohoku extension
178 km

Morioka

Joetsu line
270 km

Tohoku line
496 km

Hokuriku line
372 km

Niigata

Toyama

Nagaoka

Sendai

Sanyo line
553 km

Komatsu

HONSHU

Koriama

Hakata   Hiroshima   Okayama

Takasaki

Utsunomiya

Nagoya

Omiya Ueno

**Cross-city link
under construction**

Nagasaki

SHIKOKU

Osaka

Central **TOKYO**

KYUSHU

Tokaido line
515 km

Kagoshima

Kyushu line
249 km

0   100   200   300km

29

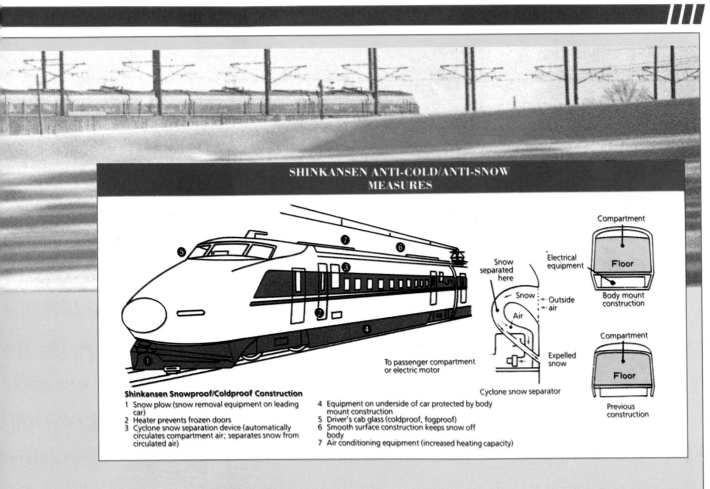

SHINKANSEN ANTI-COLD/ANTI-SNOW MEASURES

Compartment

Floor

Electrical
equipment

Snow
separated
here

Snow — Outside
air

Air

To passenger compartment
or electric motor

Expelled
snow

Cyclone snow separator

Body mount
construction

Compartment

Floor

Previous
construction

Shinkansen Snowproof/Coldproof Construction

1 Snow plow (snow removal equipment on leading car)
2 Heater prevents frozen doors
3 Cyclone snow separation device (automatically circulates compartment air; separates snow from circulated air)

4 Equipment on underside of car protected by body mount construction
5 Driver's cab glass (coldproof, fogproof)
6 Smooth surface construction keeps snow off body
7 Air conditioning equipment (increased heating capacity)

RIGHT A new 300 Series at speed. The weight of the cars was reduced from 60 to 40 tons (61 to 40.6 tonnes), thereby reducing ground vibration at high speeds. Improvements to the pantograph construction have also reduced the noise hazards of current collection.

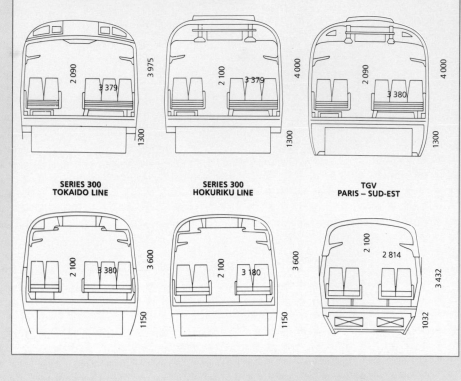

SERIES 0 — 2 090 — 3 379 — 3 975 — 1300

SERIES 100 — 2 100 — 3 379 — 4 000 — 1300

SERIES 200 — 2 090 — 3 380 — 4 000 — 1300

SERIES 300 TOKAIDO LINE — 2 100 — 3 380 — 3 600 — 1150

SERIES 300 HOKURIKU LINE — 2 100 — 3 180 — 3 600 — 1150

TGV PARIS – SUD-EST — 2 100 — 2 814 — 3 432 — 1032

BELOW **The driver's cab features monitoring devices that show operating information and the location and type of any malfunction. Vital systems such as onboard ATC (automatic train control) equipment and air-brake controls are also readily accessible.**

The later trains still retained the Bullet Train image. Known as the 200 Series, they are formed into 12-car sets, and a total of 432 cars – 36 sets – have been provided. Again all axles are driven but, because of the steeper gradients, the motor capacity has been increased to 230kW, with a corresponding increase in the capacity of the transformers, and so on. The control system now incorporates thyristors, and static converters now replace the motor-generators of the old trains. To save weight the car body shells are made from aluminium, and the seating is rather more comfortable than the early trains.

Each train set incorporates cars of seven types, including a buffet car, and arrangements are made for wheelchair passengers and other less mobile persons. The buffet car also has a pay telephone from which passengers can communicate to any part of Japan, while at the opposite end of the car there is a large wall-mounted digital speed indicator.

There is now commercial pressure to increase speeds on the Shinkansen, and the new 100 Series trains on the Tokaido line run at 240 km/h (150 mph). This has increased the average speed on the Tokyo-Hakata service to 179.7 km/h (111.7 mph). They have better aerodynamics than the earlier ones and consume about 17 per cent less energy. These train sets incorporate two double-deck vehicles in their formation, which have nine separate compartments — one for three passengers, three for two passengers and five for single passengers. The sets cost about 9 per cent more to build than their predecessors, and weigh nearly 5 per cent less, as four of the 16 vehicles have no motors.

The next generation of trains, known as the 300 Series, are designed to run at 300 km/h. This is deemed to be necessary because of increased competition from internal airlines, and again they are designed to have better fuel efficiency. As with the trend elsewhere, three-phase induction motors are used with three out of four axles motored. A speed of 300 km/h is reached in 20 km from the start in just under 12 minutes.

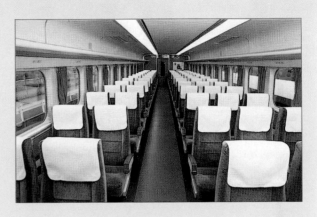

ABOVE AND BELOW The ordinary Shinkansen passenger cars all have reclining seats with armrests and facilities for the disabled. Push-button telephones are available in booths and buffets.

33

TRAIN CONTROL AND COMMUNICATION

As mentioned earlier, the Shinkansen does not employ conventional trackside signals. Instead there are two separate systems for transmitting information and communicating with trains. The driver has a visual display which tells him in effect how fast the train may travel according to route conditions. The admissible speed is governed by two things: the limit of speed imposed by physical restraints such as curvature, and the limit imposed by braking distance (governed in turn by the speed of the preceding train and/or a scheduled station stop).

The Automatic Train Control (ATC) system is the overriding factor. Should the speed of a train exceed the speed limit at any point, the ATC signal, which has the overriding control of the brakes, is transmitted to a device mounted on the train. This is achieved through a track circuit consisting of a transmission line that uses the rail as a circuit conductor.

Communication with the Control Centre is by radio telephone. For transmitting and communicating with train crews on board a "dispatcher" telephone is used. This system employs field base radio stations located about every 20 km along the line. Between five and nine stations make up one "block", and an automatic switchboard station at each block is connected to a multiplex telephone with eight channels. Two channels are for train "dispatcher" telephones and are consolidated into two circuits connected to the dispatcher booth of the Central Train Control (CTC). The remaining six channels are used for communication with the train conductor and for public telephones, and are accommodated in a train tracking device at each automatic switchboard.

The tracking device continuously monitors communications initiated in the service area of a field-base radio station and automatically switches over to the next field-base station as the train goes along the track. It is aimed to have telephone communication on more than 99.9 per cent of the whole route, with a minimum level of clear speech on 90 per cent or more. This needs a radio repeater at the portal of each tunnel, and a radio-frequency wave is radiated inside the tunnel by a cable laid through it. At the same time, the radio wave radiated from the train is picked up by the cable to give two-way communication.

Since the system was installed, coded transmissions have been adopted along with extra communication channels. To cope with this a special cable (a coaxial leakage cable) has been installed along all lines.

SHINKANSEN TODAY

By the end of 1986, five more Shinkansen schemes were under consideration. The accompanying map shows the existing and proposed lines, and indicates where small extensions are being made to existing routes. Preliminary work started on three lines before the break-up of the national railway system, and has continued since through the Japanese Railway Construction Corporation (JRCC) acting as a Government agent. The Seikan Tunnel has been completed, and the Sapporo extension of the Tohoku Shinkansen is now operating.

LEFT The general control centre is the central nervous system of the network, checking all Shinkansen operations as they happen.

ABOVE The train control centre monitors train traffic, connections with other trains as well as the speedy processing of accidents and other emergencies.

OPPOSITE The styling of the Series 300 (right) departs from the well-known bullet nose form of the Series 100 and 200 (left) and represents the culmination of aerodynamic research into drag reduction.

LATER VARIATIONS ON THE SAME THEME

During the first 23 years of Shinkansen operation a number of minor modifications were made as the result of experience. In March 1985 a new model was introduced making use of suggestions from passengers and incorporating new technology. This was the 100 Series which comes in two variants, one with a double-deck dining car; the other with a "Green" car which has a cafeteria on the lower deck and first class accommodation on the upper deck.

The new trains run as 16-car formations – the double-deck dining cars are used on the Tokyo-Hakata line and the "Green" cars on the Tokyo and Shin-Osaka run. As these new trains were introduced a corresponding number of the old trains became redundant and were eventually scrapped.

Externally the main styling change was the provision of a longer nose but internally the changes are principally designed to increase comfort and passenger amenity.

New state-of-the-art traction control equipment is provided but dc series traction motors are retained. Whereas the original trains had all axles driven the new trains have motors of larger capacity (230kW) on only 12 of the 16 cars; the two double-deck cars have no motors. The total weight of a train set is reduced to 925 tonnes in spite of the cars being slightly bigger dimensionally.

The need to reduce journey times still more has led to a further redesign and what is known as the 300 Series and is a radical departure from the first two series. Journey times on the Shin-Osaka line have come down progressively for the 515.4 km from 4 hours with the introduction in 1964 through 3 hours 10 minutes in 1965 to 2 hours 56 minutes for the 100 Series trains in 1986. The latest 300 Series trains are the result of development which commenced in 1987 and incorporate vehicles of a lower height and made from aluminium alloy to save weight. The top speed has been increased from 220 km/h (137 mph) to 270 km/h (168 mph) and to cut down air resistance at the higher speeds a totally new front-end profile has been adopted.

As a further technology change was made involving ac traction motors and regenerative braking together with a new design of bogie incorporating air springs, a series of trial runs was made commencing in the spring of 1990. A full analysis was made of noise and vibration, reliability, and overall safety together with the assimilation of data relating to car design and passenger amenity. While there are still 16 cars to each train, now only 10 are motored. Also it is planned to have only two current collectors per train instead of the eight used previously.

The first of the new trains have just entered passenger service (Spring 1992) and will cut the time still further to 2 hours 30 minutes. For the technically-minded the accompanying table sets out the differences in the three main series of trains.

IC125 AND IC225 –
BRITISH RAIL'S HIGH-SPEED TRAINS

GEC ALSTHOM

IC125: THE CONCEPT

By 1968 it became apparent that Britain needed Inter-City trains to meet a demand for prestige services with limited stops, with a high standard of comfort and able to match the French maximum speed of 200 km/h (125 mph). Gas turbine propulsion was considered, but at that time no sufficiently powerful gas turbine was available for this purpose. It was decided to stay with diesel engines and electric transmission. At the end of 1968 proposals were submitted to the Commercial and Operating Departments of British Rail for a high-speed Inter-City train consisting of seven passenger coaches of a new design (Mk 3), with a diesel-electric power car at each end. Calculations showed that, including all services requirements, a total of 3357kW (4500hp) would be needed to give good acceleration and to cover long stretches at 200 km/h (125 mph).

BELOW A 1969 model of a possible design for an HST power car with Mk3 trailers. Note the inclusion of an automatic coupler.

ABOVE Three ICI25s lined up in Paddington Station (London), from where they will leave for Cornwall, Wales and Bristol.

IMPORTANT ADAPTATIONS

The new Mk 3 coaches were designed primarily as locomotive-hauled vehicles and had to be adapted for the high-speed diesel train. The chief difference was the addition of electric cables and connections to carry the control and heating circuits between the power cars. The Mk 3 was an air-conditioned open coach with seats each side of a central gangway, and was made as long as possible within the restrictions imposed by curves and track clearances. The specified speed of 200 km/h (125 mph) would limit the axle load of each power car to 19.35 tonnes (19 tons), and only a light, quick-running engine could be accommodated. Only one such engine was at that time available from a British manufacturer – Davey Paxman – and the 12-cylinder version of this engine, the Paxman Valenta, would be able to produce the necessary 1678.5kW (2250hp).

Because of the fixed train formation, a change from the usual seating arrangement was tried, and on some experimental vehicles one-way seating was installed. Even so with conventional seating, because the size of the windows was standardized in first and second (standard) class cars, seats no longer coincided exactly with the windows. One-way seating was not popular even though it provided eight more seats in each second-class vehicle. Particular attention was given to smooth riding and low noise levels. With air-conditioning there is no point in letting passengers open windows and, as a result, fixed double-glazed windows were fitted in all but the end vestibules, where door drop-lights had to be used. Automatic doors divide the passenger section from the end vestibules.

Before this time 160 km/h (100 mph) had been the normal maximum speed, and signal spacing was based on the stopping distance of a locomotive-hauled train travelling at that speed. The most important requirement now was to be able to stop a high-speed train (HST) from 200 km/h (125 mph) within the braking distance allowed by the existing signalling. It was this factor that limited the speed of the train to 200 km/h (125 mph).

Standard British Rail air brakes are used. Coupled with disc brakes on all wheels and an additional tread-conditioning brake on the power cars, an HST can stop from 200 km/h (125 mph) in a distance slightly less than an existing locomotive-hauled train from 160 km/h (100 mph). To guard against a wheel or wheels picking up during an emergency or normal stop, a wheel-slide protection device is fitted.

To provide a comfortable ride, a new design of bogie was adopted. It is a lightweight construction with a minimum of wearing parts, using coil primary springs and air secondary springing. A new bogie design, of rather heavier construction to take the heavier vehicle and trac-

tion forces, is provided on the power cars. This has a different suspension and employs flexicoils on the secondary system.

A prototype train, known as the High Speed Diesel Train (HSDT), was authorized, and construction began in mid-1970. Although completed in June 1972, the HSDT did not begin high-speed test running until June 1973, thanks to union intransigence. During a long and intensive test programme a number of high-speed runs were made, culminating with a record speed for diesel traction of 230 km/h (143 mph) attained on the East Coast Main Line between Thirsk and Tollerton on 12 June 1973 on practically level track.

INTERCITY 125 (Britain)	
GAUGE:	4 ft 8½ in (1435 mm)
Transmission system:	Electric
FORMATION:	2+7 or 2+8
Power cars:	2
Trailer cars:	7 or 8*
BUILT:	1974–82
Builder:	BREL Crewe and Derby
Number built:	95 sets
WEIGHTS:	Complete set – 2+7: 378 tonnes (371 tons)
	2+8: 416 tonnes (408 tons)
Power car:	69.5 tonnes (68.3 tons)
Trailer car:	33.5 tonnes (33 tons)
Catering car:	36–38 tonnes (35.4–37.3 tons)
DIMENSIONS:	196 or 219 m (645 or 721 ft) overall
Power car:	17370 mm (56 ft 11½ in)
Trailer car:	23000 mm (75 ft 5½ in)
SEATING:	96/144 First, 456 Second (Standard)
POWER EQUIPMENT:	Diesel electric
Engine:	Paxman Valenta 12RP200L – 2250 hp (1678.5 kW)#
Alternator:	Brush BA1001B
TRACTION MOTORS:	4 dc series type
Type:	Brush TNH68–46 or GEC G417AZ
MAX PERMITTED SPEED:	200 km/hr (125 mph)
Normal service speed:	200 km/hr (125 mph)
BRAKING SYSTEM:	Electropneumatic
Type:	Wheel-mounted discs

* Some nine-car formations were run for a time.

\# Four power cars (43167–70) have been fitted with Mirrlees Blackstone 12MB190 engines of the same power output.

RIGHT Power car 43010 leads a 7+2 formation on the Manchester-Plymouth line in April 1987. This is the final design evolved from the models and the pre-production prototype.

Each power car of the HST has one Paxman Valenta 12-cylinder Vee turbo pressure-charged and intercooled diesel engine developing 2250hp gross at 1500 rpm. The engine is direct-coupled to a pair of Brush Electrical machine alternators, one for traction and one for the heating, air conditioning and other services. The output from the traction alternator is rectified and supplied to four dc traction motors, one to each axle driving the road wheels through flexible couplings and single-reduction gears. Engine speed and hence power is controlled by the driver in a number of steps, and an electronic regulator maintains a fixed power output corresponding to each controller position irrespective of train speed; the engine in the rear power car is remotely controlled. The diesel engine is water-cooled and the water temperature is kept more or less constant by air drawn and blown through two radiator panels, with separate circuits for the engine jacket and intercooler.

ABOVE **An HST power pack. A Paxman 12-cylinder "Valenta" engine; it is shown on its transporting cradle coupled to Brush alternators after overhaul in the Derby works. The turbocharger and intercoolers can be seen above the "Vee" formed by the two banks of cylinders.**

40

TRAIN SERVICES

The introduction of high-speed trains on the Paddington-Bristol/South Wales services heralded a new era of travel on British Rail. The first trains were introduced with a new timetable on 6 October 1976, for which 27 2+7 sets were provided. They soon settled down to provide fast and reliable services, and were well received by the travelling public. One service, the 17.20 from Paddington to Bristol, achieved a timetabled average speed of 167.9 km/h (104.3 mph) to its first stop at Chippenham, 151 km (94 miles) from London.

Following the success of the South Wales services, it was decided to replace the ageing Deltic locomotives on the London to Leeds/Newcastle/Edinburgh services. Authorization for a batch of 42 8+2 sets was sought, but this was reduced to 32 sets by the Department of Transport. This meant that some of the semi-fast services would still have to be worked by Deltic locomotives with seven or eight coaches. The full service of HSTs could not be operated until 20 August 1979 because of the disruption caused by the collapse of Penmanshields Tunnel. An interim service had started in mid-1978 as sets became available. It was now possible to travel from Kings Cross to Edinburgh in 4 hours and 43 minutes including a stop at Newcastle – an average speed of 135.7 km/h (84.3 mph). At that time there were 88 station-to-station runs at start-to-stop averages varying between 144.8 and 157 km/h (90 and 97.6 mph).

The success of the South Wales service prompted a further batch of 14 2+7 sets for the London-Plymouth-Penzance route, which began in October 1979. These were followed by a batch of 18 2+7 sets for the NE/SW cross-country services via Birmingham, commencing in the summer of 1981. A final batch of 4 trains was authorized in January 1980 for the East Coast lines, making a total of 95.

For the maintenance of the trains, new depots were built at Old Oak Common (London), Bristol (St Philips Marsh), Plymouth (Laira), Bounds Green (London), Newcastle (Heaton), Leeds (Nevill Hill) and Edinburgh (Craigentinny). Each depot has sections for normal cleaning, refuelling and maintenance and repair work, and can accommodate full-length trains of nine or ten vehicles as appropriate on one road, under cover. One of the principal features of the Mark 3 vehicles is the modular

THE INTERCITY NETWORK

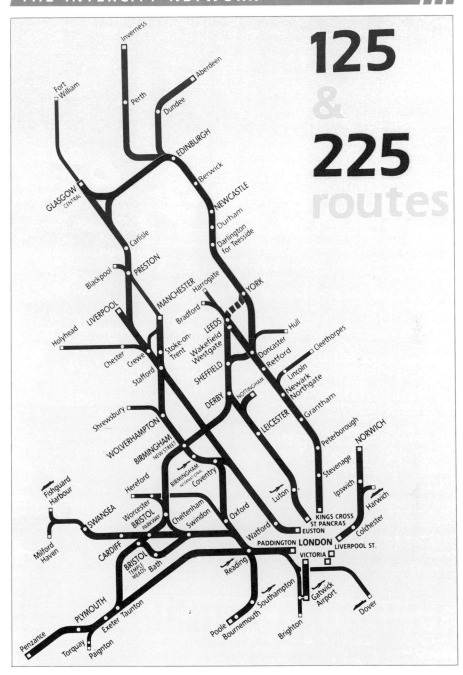

125 & 225 routes

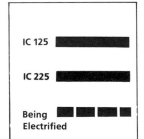

IC 125

IC 225

Being Electrified

41

design of the undercar equipment, which considerably eases the maintenance man's work. Although the farings extend downwards towards rail level, easily opened doors reveal the various modules which can be withdrawn, unplugged and replaced for maintenance or in case of failure.

Electrification of the London-Edinburgh/Leeds lines has now released a number of HST sets which have been allocated to other services to replace locomotive-hauled trains, such as Manchester-Poole/Weymouth and through trains from places such as Penzance to Aberdeen.

British Rail's high-speed train concept was relatively conventional, but even in 1976 it made use of develop-

ing hi-tech electronics with plug-in replaceable modules in the traction control and braking functions. New and improved materials were employed in its construction. Particularly interesting were the driver's cabs, which were built as a complete unit in resin-bonded fibreglass. One worry was the damage that might be caused by striking a solid object at 200 km/h (125 mph). Special tests were made with various thicknesses of material and of the glass for the front windows, with extremely satisfactory results. Today British Rail still operates the fastest diesel-powered trains in the world, and will continue to do so for the rest of this century.

THE AUSTRALIAN CONNECTION

HST technology was sold by British Rail to the New South Wales State Railway Authority and is used on its so-called XS project.

TECHNICAL DETAILS

Technically XPT is an improved and adapted version of the British HST. The standard formation is two power cars and five trailers. Built in Australia by Comeng in corrugated stainless steel, the passenger cars demonstrate the most obvious departure from British practice. They are just under 4 ft longer than the British Mk 3 cars, with a body length of 24.2 m (79 ft 4¾ in) for the same number of second-class seats. The standard of comfort is higher. The BT10 bogie was modified to suit Australian track, but retains the same suspension principles.

Several design improvements were made to the power cars which are 442 mm (17.4 in) shorter than the originals and some 2.5 tonnes (5500 lb) lighter. The Australian engineers claimed that weight distribution was better than the British version. The same Paxman Valenta engine is used, but de-rated to 2000hp (principally to offset the effects of higher operating temperatures). Also the smaller number of cars and lower top speed do not warrant the full 2250hp of the HSTs.

Rather than being the predicted failure, the XPT has been such a success that extra cars and sets have been required. But all has not been plain sailing, and the volatility of the Australian labour unions has led to some unplanned changes. Immediately the first trains were delivered there was a dispute with the unions over the lack of guard's accommodation. This resulted in an order for five additional passenger cars with enlarged guard/luggage compartments, which were delivered from Comeng in late 1983. In the first trains the guard had a small area next to the galley in the Type-2 car.

In 1984 Comeng delivered a further five power cars and 10 passenger coaches which, together with the extra passenger/guard's cars made up six 2+5 sets for revenue-earning service, leaving three power cars and five passenger cars spare. This was the situation until 1985 when SRA ordered a further 12 passenger cars to increase the six sets to the 2+7 formation.

A purpose-built maintenance depot was constructed at Sydney, 5 km (3 miles) south of the terminal station. The depot deals with all running maintenance, facilitated by having the spare vehicles. Although XPTs nominally run as fixed formations, individual vehicles are often taken out of sets for maintenance and are replaced by ones from the pool of spares.

There is no doubt that XPT has made a positive impact, despite controversy on the fare structure, seating and catering. The XPT's amenities and faster service (still rela-

XPT (Australia)	
GAUGE: Transmission	Standard 4 ft 8½ in (1435 mm) Electric
FORMATION: Power cars: Trailers:	2+5 (later some 2+6) 2 5 (some 6)
BUILT: Builder: Number built: Service requirement:	1980–85 Comeng 15 power and 35 assorted trailer cars 6 sets
DIMENSIONS: Power car: Trailer car:	155 m (510 ft) overall 16932 mm (55 ft 6½ in) 24200 mm (79 ft 4¾ in)
SEATING: Type 1: Type 2: Type 3:	Variable according to formation 72 64 plus galley and guard's compartment 40 plus buffet car
POWER EQUIPMENT: Engine: Alternator:	Diesel electric Ruston Paxman Valenta 12RP200L – 2000 hp, 1500 rpm Brush BA1001B
TRACTION MOTORS: Type:	4 dc series type Brush TNH68–46
MAX PERMITTED SPEED: Normal service speed:	160 km/hr (100 mph) 160 km/hr max

tively slow by British HST standards) have given impetus to an increase in passengers. On 14 May 1986 the NSW Minister for Transport announced that 14 new high-performance trains (HPT) would be introduced between then and 1996.

POLITICAL FALL-OUT

XPT has been described as a "political" train. In the early 1980s the State Railway Authority (SRA) of New South Wales was undergoing a major revival. Passenger traffic in the years 1975-79 had increased by 14 per cent and freight tonnage by 27 per cent. The SRA claimed that after years of neglect and decline, railways were on the way up. That view was not universally shared by the press or public. The way to get the message across was to have something tangible, and in 1979 the NSW Transport Commission announced that instead of ordering more locomotive-hauled rolling stock it was going for Inter-City XPT trains based on the British HST. This to the Australians was rather like the British Transport Secretary announcing that he was to buy French TGVs to solve a problem on a particular line of British Rail.

The SRA countered its critics by saying that even with a top speed of 160 km/h (100 mph), the much greater acceleration and braking would significantly reduce journey times between Sydney and the country centres. With the state elections due in September 1981, XPT became the target for much political in-fighting between the state premier and the opposition. When the first two vehicles – a power car and one trailer – were handed over with a blaze of publicity on 24 August 1981, there was a large crowd present. The two cars toured New South Wales between then and election day (19 September 1981), attracting large crowds at each stop. As a final fling the Country Party claimed that the train would never reach 140 km/h (87 mph), let alone 160 km/h (100 mph). In reply the SRA mounted a series of test runs with one power car, two trailers and a test van during which, in the course of several runs, speeds in excess of 160 km/h were attained.

The state premier was re-elected and immediately announced his party's firm intention to produce "plenty more from where this came from".

OPPOSITE The Australian version of British Rail's IC125 in its new colours. The similarity of the styling is immediately apparent.

BELOW The XPT displaying its original livery in a snowy South Wales setting. Poor weather adversely affects rail transport the world over.

43

IC225 – EAST COAST ELECTRICS

Mention was made earlier about releasing IC125 sets to other services following the electrification of the East Coast main line from London to Edinburgh and Glasgow. From the time of British Rail's modernization plan of 1955, electrification of the East Coast main line had been the preferred option.

A number of proposals had been made, but the advent of the IC125 made the financial case for electrification difficult to prove. For a while British Rail's operators seemed to be content with the journey times between London and Edinburgh or London and Leeds that were achieved within a maximum speed of 200 km/h (125 mph). With the rapid development of electric traction and by adopting different operating methods, it was clear that a time of 4 hours was practical between London and Edinburgh. The East Coast main line has only slight gradients, is relatively straight – at least south of the

ABOVE Clean layout of instruments and operating comfort are the hallmarks of the class 91 locomotive. This is the "front" cab; the one at the rear has a similar layout, but the windows are vertical.

BELOW A class 91 locomotive at the head of train of Mk4 coaches with a driving van trailer at the rear. The class 91 normally leads the trains when travelling north.

44

EQUIPMENT LAYOUT OF CLASS 91 LOCOMOTIVES

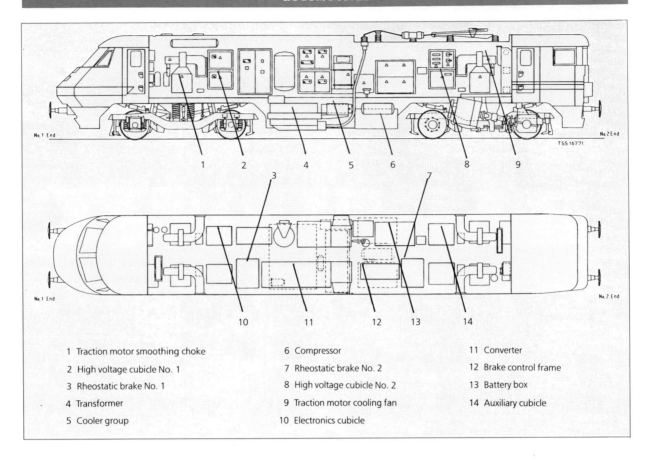

1 Traction motor smoothing choke	6 Compressor	11 Converter
2 High voltage cubicle No. 1	7 Rheostatic brake No. 2	12 Brake control frame
3 Rheostatic brake No. 1	8 High voltage cubicle No. 2	13 Battery box
4 Transformer	9 Traction motor cooling fan	14 Auxiliary cubicle
5 Cooler group	10 Electronics cubicle	

45

border between England and Scotland – and connects few major centres of population. In short it is ideally suited to high-speed operation, as had already been shown by the successful use of the IC125. With new technical developments it was clear that savings could be made on the fixed equipment, overhead lines and signalling. On 27 July 1984 electrification was at last authorized.

Thirty-one new high-power four-axle electric locomotives, Class 91, and matching sets of new Mk 4 rolling stock have been built. They have a potential for 225 km/h (140 mph). Locomotives and coaches are marshalled into standard formations of 10 vehicles, with the locomotive at one end and a Driving Van Trailer at the other. This method of operation (push-pull) is not a new concept. As long ago as 1967, the principle of propelling eight or more vehicles at speeds of up to 145 km/h (90 mph) had been adopted for the London-Bournemouth line. It was also adopted for the APT, which ran many hundreds of miles at 200 km/h (125 mph) or more. Research and practical tests had shown there was no problem in extending the principle to even higher speeds.

Wiring had to be installed from Hitchin to Leeds, Newcastle and Edinburgh – the stretch between London (Kings Cross) and Hitchin (51.5 km, or 32 miles) had

been electrified for suburban services in 1977. With more than 25 years of experience, it was carried out very much more cheaply, and with less environmental impact, than the parallel line between London (Euston), Birmingham, Manchester and Liverpool.

Electric trains began to run to Leeds on 11 August 1988, the full high-speed service commencing in October 1989 and to Edinburgh in May 1991. They set new standards of high-speed running in Britain. At a special demonstration on 26 September 1991, locomotive 91012, with a load of six vehicles weighing 265 tonnes (260 tons), ran the 632.6 km (393.1 miles) non-stop from London (King's Cross) to Edinburgh in 3 hours 29 minutes at an average speed of 181.6 km/h (112.85 mph). The maximum speed of 225 km/h (140 mph) was attained over a total distance of 236.6 km (147 miles), while a further 294.5 km (183 miles) were run at speeds between 209 and 225 km/h (130-140 mph). Six hours was allowed in 1938 with the steam-hauled Coronation, which rarely exceeded 160 km/h (100 mph). From 30 September 1991, there was a regular service from London to Edinburgh, calling at York and Newcastle, covering the distance in 3 hours 59 minutes – an average speed of 158.8 km/h (98.7 mph).

THE COACHES

Mk 4 coaches are built to a profile, like the SNCF Grand Confort coaches, which permits "tilt" to be added at a later date if required. The locomotive profile matches but is not, as with the Swedish X2 locomotives, built to tilt (see Chapter 6). The vehicles, built by Metro Cammell (now part of GEC), are the same length as the Mk 3 but run on Schlieren-designed bogies. These too have been subjected to the most stringent riding tests and had to be adjusted before acceptance by British Rail.

It is interesting to reflect that the locomotives were ready before the coaches, and prior to full operation were run with rakes of Mk 3 vehicles. To enable push-pull operation, 10 HSTs were used. One power car was removed and replaced by a Class 91 locomotive. The other power car was modified, the external appearance being altered by the addition of side buffers.

Internally, a TDM system was installed, operating over the existing control cables, allowing the Class 91 to be controlled from the HST cab. Because the HST auxiliary power supply was not compatible with that from the Class 91, the train auxiliaries, air conditioning, and so on were fed from the diesel generator set of the HST power car. Traction power was also available from the HST power car in case of need!

As rakes of Mk 4 vehicles became available during 1989, they replaced the part-HST sets which were re-deployed on other services. Full electric operation between London and Leeds was available from October 1989 onwards.

HSTs still operate over parts of the East Coast main line on cross-country workings from the West Country, and of course on through services to Aberdeen and Inverness, Cleethorpes, Hull, and so on.

INTERCITY 225 (Britain)	
GAUGE:	4 ft 8½ in (1435 mm)
System:	25kV ac 50hz
FORMATION:	1+10
Locomotive:	1
Trailers:	9
Driving van trailer:	1
BUILT:	GEC/BREL
Locomotive:	BREL as sub-contractor to GEC (Crewe)
Trailer:	GEC Birmingham
Driving van trailer:	GEC Birmingham
Number built:	31 sets
WEIGHTS:	Complete train 476 tonnes (468.5 tons)
Locomotive:	81.5 tonnes (80 tons)
Trailer:	40 tonnes (39.4 tons)
Driving van trailer:	34.5 tonnes (33.9 tons)
DIMENSIONS:	23000 mm (75 ft 5½ in) long
Width:	2740 mm (8 ft 11¾ in)
SEATING:	508 but can vary
First:	46 per vehicle
Standard:	74 per vehicle
LOCOMOTIVE:	Class 91
Wheel arrangement:	Bo-Bo
Rating:	4530 kW (6075 hp)
Peak output:	4700 kW (6300 hp)
Motors:	4 dc separately-excited
Type:	GEC 426AZ
Maximum speed:	225 km/hr (140 mph)
Maximum load:	830 tonnes at 160 km/hr
Length:	19400 mm (63 ft 7¾ in)
Width:	2740 mm (8ft 11¾ in)
Bogie centres:	10500 mm (34 ft 5½ in)
Wheel diameter:	1000 mm (3 ft 3¼ in)
Control system:	Microprocessor-controlled Thryistor
Braking:	Rheostatic 225 to 45 km/hr (28 mph) Shaft-mounted disc and tread to standstill

ABOVE The Mk4 body shell shown on "accommodation" bogies prior to being fitted out. Note the wide gangway and the sliding plug doors.

BELOW View of the interior of a Mk4 first-class coach. The normal 2+1 seating is employed, and the seats have limited adjustment.

IC225 LOCOMOTIVES

The 31 new Class 91 electric locomotives were supplied by GEC to a very stringent specification, which included a guaranteed period of trouble-free running before being taken over by British Rail. The mechanical parts were built and the equipment erected in the former British Rail works at Crewe, now owned by BREL. These locomotives are examples of the latest in high technology and are designed to haul and propel trains of up to 520 tonnes (510 tons) at speeds of up to 225 km/h (140 mph). They weigh 81.5 tonnes (80 tons) and develop 4530kW (6075hp).

The Class 91 has four separately-excited dc motors mounted in the locomotive body and driving the axles through Cardan shafts and axle-mounted right-angle gear boxes. A disc brake is mounted on an extension of each motor shaft. Electric rhoestatic braking is also provided, and used from the highest speed

down to a level where the disc brakes are blended in to take over as the rheostatic brake fades to zero. The electrical energy generated by the motors is dissipated in resistances. Power is regulated in a thyristor converter controlled by microprocessor.

The locomotives are unusual for Europe in having an asymmetric shape. They are normally marshalled at the northern end of trains, so one cab only has a wedge-streamlined form. Streamlining of the other end of the train is provided by a similar form on the Driving Van Trailer (DVT). This is a vehicle with a driving cab and full controls from which the locomotive is operated when pushing the train. Control of the locomotive is achieved electronically along a pair of wires that run the length of the train. Between the DVT and the locomotive there are normally eight of the new Mk 4 coaches.

RIGHT At the opposite end of the train to the locomotive, control is provided from a driver's cab in the driving van trailer. This picture shows a DVT under construction and illustrates the similarity of end styling to that of the locomotive.

BELOW An IC225 locomotive with the majestic backdrop of York Minster. This point is now less than 2½ hours' travelling time from London.

ICE –
GERMANY'S INTER-CITY EXPRESS

A designer's prototype of a streamlined ICE power car. The train is depicted on a section of upgraded "normal" line.

The West German politicians' belief in railways in the 1980s (and subsequently) is in striking contrast to that of the British Cabinet, not least the visceral distaste for rail travel publicly expressed by the former British Prime Minister, Margaret Thatcher.

FINANCE AND FORWARD-THINKING

In the West German Federal Transport Plan, the *Bundesverkehrswegeplanung* (BVWP), a very large sum of money was budgeted for railways. The creation of some new very high-speed lines, Neubaustrecke (NBS), and the upgrading with automatic train control equipment of many existing routes, Ausbaustrecke (ABS), were given priority. In 1986 terms, by which time work was well in hand with the initial NBS, a total of the equivalent of £10.4 billion had been committed.

The cost of the new NBS lines is inflated by the very high cost of making them environmentally unobtrusive for the operation of new Inter-City Express trains at 250 km/h (155 mph) with a potential of 280 km/h (174 mph). At the same time there was still a belief that Germany's Transrapid Maglev system would be chosen for at least one route between two major cities. Trans-

rapid is certainly not unobtrusive, because it uses an unsightly elevated guideway. So far it has been beset by problems and is not yet ready (as discussed in more detail in a later chapter).

Inter-City Express is now a reality. Two lengths of NBS were inaugurated in 1991 from Hannover to Wurzburg and Mannheim to Stuttgart, a total length of 430 km (267 miles). The Hannover-Wurzburg line forms an important part of the Hamburg-Munich trunk route and, unlike France's TGV, is routed through stations on the classic lines at important junctions, serving places such as Gottingen, Kassel and Fulda. This has involved a number of expensive civil engineering works, with flyovers and flyunders designed to give the NBS tracks a clear path. It is as well to remember that all of the major Deutsche Bundesbahn infra-structure projects, including electrification, are federally funded.

To add to the two lines just opened, the Cologne to Frankfurt NBS is under construction. It is proposed to split the line at Eddersheim, between Wiesbaden and Frankfurt, so as to serve Frankfurt Airport, already provided with a three-track station handling 7.5 million passengers a year. A new station is planned to the east of the present station, and is expected to be completed by 1997. Until the new station is finished IC-Expresses will use the existing station. The Hannover-Wurzburg line is

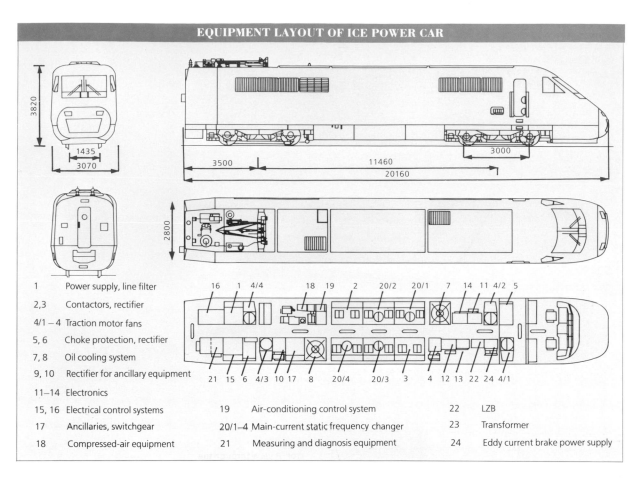

1	Power supply, line filter	
2,3	Contactors, rectifier	
4/1 – 4	Traction motor fans	
5, 6	Choke protection, rectifier	
7, 8	Oil cooling system	
9, 10	Rectifier for ancillary equipment	
11–14	Electronics	
15, 16	Electrical control systems	
17	Ancillaries, switchgear	
18	Compressed-air equipment	
19	Air-conditioning control system	22 LZB
20/1–4	Main-current static frequency changer	23 Transformer
21	Measuring and diagnosis equipment	24 Eddy current brake power supply

50

326 km (203 miles) long and cuts through mountains and across deep valleys. Again unlike the French TGV, it is designed for mixed traffic, including fast freight, and has a minimum curve radius of 7000 m (23,030 feet) and a ruling gradient of 1 in 80 (1.25 per cent). The conse-quence of this is some 34 km (21 miles) of bridges and 62 tunnels totalling 116 km (72 miles) – one of which, the Landrucken tunnel south of Fulda, is 10.75 km (6.5 miles) long. It is near the summit of the line which is 386 m (1270 feet) above sea level.

RIGHT The characteristics of the Neubaustrecke are here clearly shown, as one of the new trains crosses a reinforced concrete viaduct having just emerged from a tunnel under the hill in the background.

LEFT Illustration of one of the asynchronous, three-phase traction motors. Unlike both TGV and IC225 (British Rail Class 91) the motors are mounted within the bogie frames.

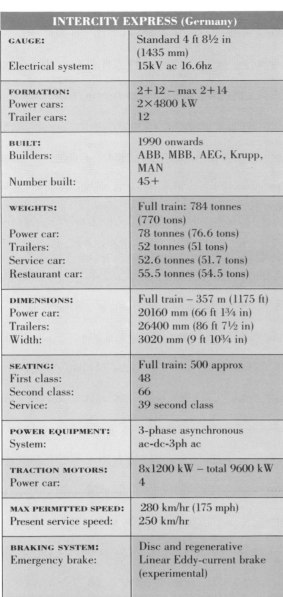

INTERCITY EXPRESS (Germany)	
GAUGE:	Standard 4 ft 8½ in (1435 mm)
Electrical system:	15kV ac 16.6hz
FORMATION:	2+12 – max 2+14
Power cars:	2×4800 kW
Trailer cars:	12
BUILT:	1990 onwards
Builders:	ABB, MBB, AEG, Krupp, MAN
Number built:	45+
WEIGHTS:	Full train: 784 tonnes (770 tons)
Power car:	78 tonnes (76.6 tons)
Trailers:	52 tonnes (51 tons)
Service car:	52.6 tonnes (51.7 tons)
Restaurant car:	55.5 tonnes (54.5 tons)
DIMENSIONS:	Full train – 357 m (1175 ft)
Power car:	20160 mm (66 ft 1¾ in)
Trailers:	26400 mm (86 ft 7½ in)
Width:	3020 mm (9 ft 10¾ in)
SEATING:	Full train: 500 approx
First class:	48
Second class:	66
Service:	39 second class
POWER EQUIPMENT:	3-phase asynchronous
System:	ac-dc-3ph ac
TRACTION MOTORS:	8x1200 kW – total 9600 kW
Power car:	4
MAX PERMITTED SPEED:	280 km/hr (175 mph)
Present service speed:	250 km/hr
BRAKING SYSTEM:	Disc and regenerative
Emergency brake:	Linear Eddy-current brake (experimental)

TOP A view through the driver's cab windows. The two VDUs can clearly be seen, together with the excellent layout of instruments, switches and indicators.

ABOVE A view of a power car bogie. The two traction motors can be seen near the centre of the bogie between the two sets of secondary flexicoil springs. The drive is taken through double-reduction gears to each axle.

51

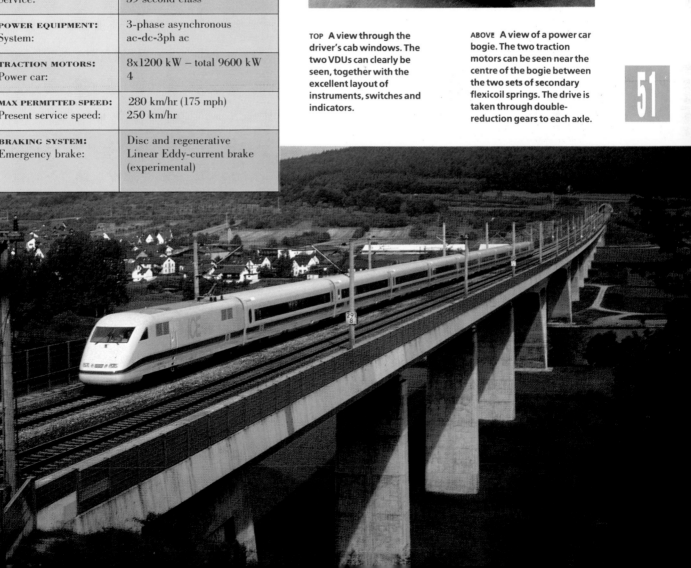

THE TRAINS

The forerunner of the IC-Express train sets was an experimental 5-unit train set, known as the Intercity-experimental (ICE), which was first demonstrated to the public towards the end of 1985 during the celebrations of the 150th anniversary of the German Railways. The train was a joint development between the rail industry and the German Federal Railways (Deutsche Bundesbahnen), and was substantially financed by the Federal Ministry of Research and Technology (BMFT). The following objectives had to be met:

1. to investigate and test operation on specially prepared test lines at speeds up to 350 km/h (217 mph).
2. to demonstrate the ability to run with normal speeds up to 300 km/h (186 mph).

The five-vehicle train consisted of two identical streamlined power cars, two intermediate trailers with variable interior layouts, and a dynamometer car for technical records and measurements. The planned very high operating speeds made aerodynamic shape of importance in keeping energy consumption within bounds. And because a significant proportion of each new line would be in tunnels, it was equally important to reduce the effect of one train passing another at a closing speed of 500 km/h (310 mph) or more. The results of the tests are amply demonstrated in the production trains, where the pressure sealing, if very expensive, is extremely effective.

Every aspect of the proposed new trains was extensively tested both on the line and in a special roller-rig at Munich. The first high-speed public demonstration was on 26 November 1985, when a speed of 317 km/h (197 mph) was attained. A year later on 17 November 1986 this was increased to 345 km/h (214 mph). This heralded a two-week examination of public opinion to test reactions to a number of special features. The ICE was run on the inter-city lines between Frankfurt-Munich and Frankfurt-Hannover when a representative group of passengers was asked for their views about comfort, design, passenger information systems and transfer of luggage. The answers were extremely valuable in finalizing the design of the production trains. It was also a useful marketing exercise to estimate the chances of winning passengers from other modes of transport. "Twice as fast as the car, half as fast as the plane" is the often repeated claim of Deutsche Bundesbahn's ex-airline marketing manager.

Following the ICE came the first 45 production train sets. The present makeup has two 4800kW power cars weighing 78 tonnes (171,600 lb), one at each end of eleven trailer cars. The power cars are driven by four asynchronous three-phase traction motors. There are

BELOW **The picture shows a 2 + 13 formation on part of the Neubaustrecke, running alongside a main road. The fifth trailer from the rear is the "service" vehicle.**

THE ICE NETWORK IIII

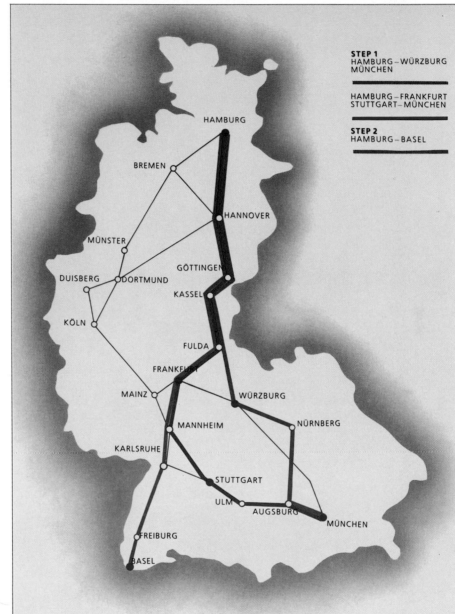

STEP 1
HAMBURG – WÜRZBURG
MÜNCHEN

HAMBURG – FRANKFURT
STUTTGART – MÜNCHEN

STEP 2
HAMBURG – BASEL

HAMBURG
BREMEN
HANNOVER
MÜNSTER
GÖTTINGEN
DUISBERG
DORTMUND
KASSEL
KÖLN
FULDA
FRANKFURT
MAINZ
WÜRZBURG
MANNHEIM
NÜRNBERG
KARLSRUHE
STUTTGART
ULM
AUGSBURG
MÜNCHEN
FREIBURG
BASEL

53

three first-class cars, one restaurant/bistro, one service/ special compartment car and six second-class cars, although power is sufficient for the addition of another two trailer cars – to make 15 vehicles in all. The total weight of the present set, without passengers and luggage, is 732 tonnes (719 tons) and the maximum design speed in service is 280 km/h (174 mph) for which the NBS lines are engineered. But for the time being the IC-Express timetables are based on a limit of 250 km/h (155 mph). Later, when sufficient experience has been gained, drivers will be permitted to use the higher speed to regain any time that may have been lost.

The traction control system is based on that developed by Brown Boveri and used in the latest DB Class 120

OVER **Line-up of ICE trains at the maintenance depot. A new purpose-built depot has been provided which will service ICE only.**

THE ETR450 TRAINS

Following the demonstration run it was announced that a 90 billion lire ($63 m/£36 m) contract had been placed with Fiat for four 11-car tilting body train sets, to be classified as ETR450. Ten of the eleven cars would have traction motors – only the bar/kitchen car being a trailer. Later the order was altered to ten 11-car sets and four five-car sets, each exclusively first class. The order was again modified, and by the beginning of 1990 there were 14 eight-car ETR450s in service. In late 1989 it was decided to fit out the unmotorized bar/kitchen cars with seats and make the sets up to nine cars. Seats were provided and an area fitted out with pay telephones. There is now a meals-at-seat service provided from galleys. This last alteration left two two-car units of the original order spare. At the end of 1989 Fiat received an order for a further two twin-sets and a trailer, to make the total up to 15 nine-car sets.

The car profiles and much of the technology follow that of the ETR401 prototype. The cars have aluminium bodies and are mounted on two bogies of advanced

62

TOP **Detail of the control desk, showing on-board signal repetition unit and ground train and intercom telephones in the foreground.**

ABOVE **The airline-type seats are all reclining, and each seat-back holds a fold-down tray and magazine pouch.**

BELOW **The vehicle bogie is an original design feature and incorporates radial steering of the wheel sets. The driving vehicle bogies also feature wheel flange lubricators, signal pick-up, gyroscope sensors and anti-skid devices.**

ETR450 (Italy)	
GAUGE:	Standard 4 ft 8½ in (1435 mm)
Electrical system:	3000V dc
FORMATION:	8+1
Power cars:	8
Trailer car:	1
BUILT:	1988–
Builder:	Fiat, ABB
Number built:	15
WEIGHTS:	Complete train: 430 tonnes (422 tons)
Motor coaches:	50 tonnes (49.1 tons)
Trailer car:	30 tonnes (29.5 tons)
DIMENSIONS:	242 m (794 ft 3½ in) overall
Motor and trailer car:	26900 mm (88 ft 3 in)
SEATING:	344 (one class)
POWER EQUIPMENT:	Thyristor Chopper
System:	3000V dc
TRACTION MOTORS:	16×312.5 kW – total 5000 kW
Power car:	1 per bogie
MAX PERMITTED SPEED:	250 km/hr (155 mph)
Service speed:	250 km/hr (155 mph)
BRAKING SYSTEM:	Air and rheostatic
Electric brake capacity:	7800 kW

design, with a wheelbase of 2450 mm (8 ft ½ in). The eight motored cars of a set each carry two 312.5kW traction motors, which drive the inner axles of each bogie through Cardan shafts. Each motorized two-car unit is electrically and operationally inseparable, and weighs 93 tonnes (205,030 lb). For sustained contact and to avoid electrical arcing, only two twin-units in a nine-car set have current collectors (pantographs), and they have one to each car.

Because the cars tilt and the top of the car body moves relative to the contact wire, each pantograph is carried on a bogie-supported frame. On the prototype ETR401 train the tilt mechanism of each car was independent. The ETR450's electrically-controlled tilt system processes signals from a gyroscope and accelerometers, and sensors on the leading car transmit impulses down the train to modules on each following vehicle in the formation. These impulses command their car's own hydraulic tilt mechanisms accordingly. Body-tilt is powered hydraulically, and each bogie carries two cylinders between its cross members and anchors in the body frame.

Although the ETR450 is designed to tilt up to 10 degrees, it is at present limited to 8 degrees. The design maximum speed is 250 km/h (155 mph), and this can be exploited fully on the Rome-Florence Direttissima. On other lines, for example the predominantly straight Bologna-Turin main line, it is cleared to run at a maximum of 200 km/h (125 mph).

To enable the ETR450 to stop in acceptable distances, two braking systems are employed – disc and electric (rheostatic). The rheostatic brake has a maximum power of 1900kW, generated by the traction motors, which is dissipated in resistances as heat. As is normal with modern trains, there is a comprehensive monitoring and diagnostic system for the equipment.

Since 1989 Fiat Ferroviaria has been engaged on a second-generation ETR450 development programme. While the tilting principle remains substantially the same, improvements include traction equipment of greater power to allow more unpowered trailers per set; simplification of components for reduced maintenance and increased life; improved diagnostic systems; and a completely restyled driver's cab with more modern features.

At the same time, the German Railways (DB) borrowed the ETR401 and carried out trials to see what advantage could be gained by introducing tilting-body trains on some secondary main lines. They came to the conclusion that they could be used with advantage on the Nurnberg-Beyreuth/Hof lines where, combined with compensation of cant deficiency, the maximum speed through curves could be increased by 25 per cent. The new VT10 two-car diesel-electric railcars now being built are for 160 km/h (100 mph). They have a maximum tilt angle of 8 degrees and the bogies, tilting mechanism and its control system are identical to the Italian ETR450's.

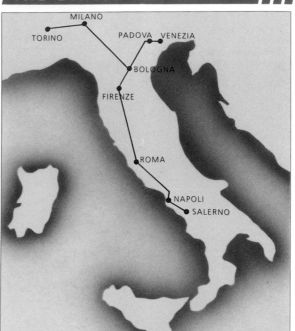

THE ETR450 NETWORK

BELOW Compared to the ETR450, the earlier British APT-E had many more unconventional features: hydrodynamic braking, a greater degree of tilt as well as novel articulation between vehicles. The project was abandoned because of shortage of funds.

SWEDISH TILTING-BODY ELECTRIC TRAINS – X2

Sweden is a country whose rail network is characterized by frequent curves. Service speeds are limited to moderate levels for conventional rolling stock. For any worthwhile improvement in journey times, new hi-tech vehicles are necessary and these must be equipped with tilting bodies if speeds through the curves are to be increased.

Investigation showed that a realistic maximum speed was about 200 km/h (125 mph), and speeds through curves could be increased by about 25-30 per cent if suitable tilting-body vehicles could be produced. For the Stockholm-Gothenburg line, the total cost of improving the vehicles and infrastructure was estimated at 2 billion Swedish Krone. A new high-speed line with the corresponding rolling stock would cost approximately 9 billion. The appropriate decision was not difficult.

THE X2 TRAIN SETS

Train sets are made up of a power car, four intermediate trailers and a driving trailer. A flexible train formation is possible by replacing the driving trailer car with another power car and additional intermediate trailers. The whole can be operated with only one current collector (pantograph).

There are only two types of intermediate trailer: a service car with almost all the special facilities needed, such as a kitchen, service compartment, buffet, and so

ROLLING STOCK: SPECIAL FEATURES

1. An active tilting-body system to enable curves to be negotiated 25-30 per cent faster without adverse effects on passenger comfort.
2. A "soft" self-steering radial-axle bogie, generating low guiding forces even at higher speeds in curves.
3. Asynchronous traction, producing the necessary tractive force with lightweight motors and a high degree of reliability.

on; and a standard seating car. The latter can easily be transformed from first to second class (and vice versa) as required. As a first-class car, it has seats for 51 passengers. As a second-class car, it holds 76 passengers. The driving trailer has seats for 49 second-class passengers and space for one wheelchair, while the service car has seats for 29 second-class passengers and a further 11 places for eating. Full dimensional details are given in the accompanying table.

Each power car has four ac three-phase asynchronous traction motors, each with a capacity of 815kW. Swedish Railways (SJ) are electrified on single-phase ac at a frequency of 16.6Hz at 15,000 volts. The control system employs the now popular GTO thyristor bridges and, combined with three-phase induction motors, allows full

RIGHT While the tilting principle of the X2000 trains is similar to that of the ETR450, it is much less complex and has proved more successful. It is based on the principle of rotational movement between the bogie frame and a beam which supports the car body.

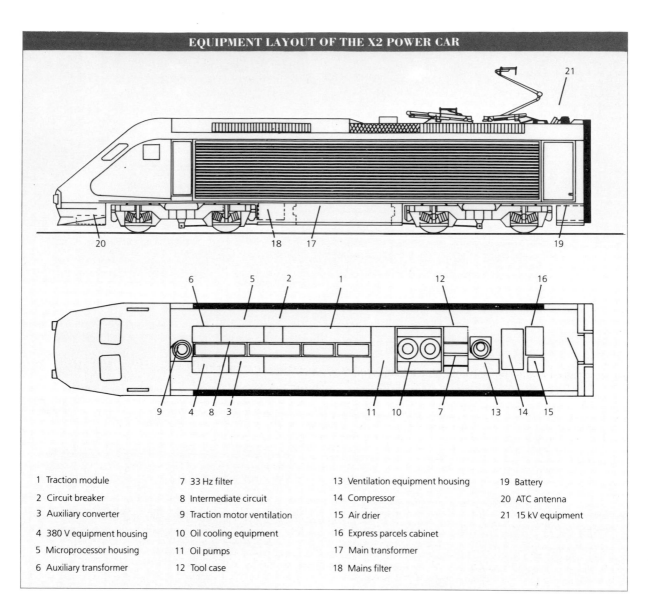

1 Traction module	7 33 Hz filter	13 Ventilation equipment housing	19 Battery
2 Circuit breaker	8 Intermediate circuit	14 Compressor	20 ATC antenna
3 Auxiliary converter	9 Traction motor ventilation	15 Air drier	21 15 kV equipment
4 380 V equipment housing	10 Oil cooling equipment	16 Express parcels cabinet	
5 Microprocessor housing	11 Oil pumps	17 Main transformer	
6 Auxiliary transformer	12 Tool case	18 Mains filter	

regenerative braking, feeding the braking energy back into the line. The maximum permitted speed is 210 km/h (130 mph).

All vehicles with passenger accommodation are equipped with a tilt mechanism. To develop this, an experimental train called X15 was built. It was a three-car electric multiple-unit set converted from a 1948 train set, and all three cars were provided with tilting equipment. The two outer cars had a pneumatically-operated system, while the centre car had a new hydraulically-operated type. The hydraulic system proved to be markedly superior. The whole system is very much less complex than the ETR450's, and is based on the principle of rotational movement between the bogie frame and a beam which supports the car body. An accelerometer on the leading bogie of the power car establishes the required angle of tilt, which is initiated through a TRACS computer. To ensure that passengers are not disturbed and nausea is minimized, the rate of tilt is limited to 4 degrees per second.

The stainless steel vehicles are fairly conventional. The trailer cars are 24,950 mm (81 ft 10¼ in) long, the driving trailers 22,255 mm (73 ft) long and the power cars 17,255 mm (56 ft 7¼ in) long. The first commercial trials began on 4 September 1990 between Stockholm and Gothenburg, when only the section of line between Hallsberg and Skovde (about 110 km/68 miles) was ready for a speed of 200 km/h. In March 1991, when the whole line had been upgraded, the time for the journey between the two cities was reduced to 2 hours 59 minutes.

It is 18 years since the X15 project began. Now 20 X2 sets have been ordered, and it is expected that ten will be operating all traffic on the Gothenburg line by the middle of 1992. The second batch of trains is destined for the Stockholm-Malmö line, and all should be running by the summer of 1994, with a time of 4 hours 10 minutes between the two cities.

The vehicle bogies are particularly novel and incorporate radial steering of the wheel-sets. Power and trailer

RIGHT X2000 trains consist of a push-pull power unit and five coaches. All passenger coaches, including the driving van trailer, are equipped with car-body tilting for improved comfort.

X2 VEHICLE BOGIES

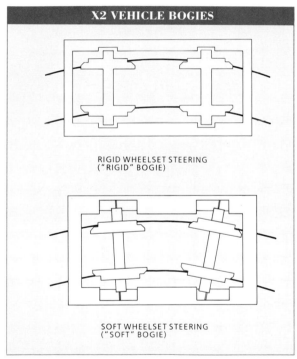

RIGID WHEELSET STEERING ("RIGID" BOGIE)

SOFT WHEELSET STEERING ("SOFT" BOGIE)

bogies are fitted with "soft" self-steering radial axles. Radial steering is achieved by the interaction between wheel conicity (all railway wheels have tyres with a conical profile) and the longitudinal friction forces. The principle is illustrated in the accompanying diagrams. While it is mechanically simple, the amount of mathematical and experimental analysis necessary to perfect a suitable design was considerable. Special laterally-soft primary springing has been developed, and secondary springing is provided by the familiar air springs.

X2000 (Sweden)	
GAUGE: Electrical system:	Standard 15kV ac 16.6hz
FORMATION: Power car: Trailer cars:	1+5 1 5
BUILT: Builder: Number built:	1989– ASEA (now ABB) 20+
WEIGHTS: Power car: Trailer car:	Complete train: 343 tonnes (337 tons) 70 tonnes (68.75 tons) 54.5 tonnes (53.5 tons)
DIMENSIONS: Power car: Trailer car: Driving van trailer:	140 m (459 ft 4 in) 17255 mm (56 ft 7½ in) 24950 mm (81 ft 10¼ in) 22255 mm (73 ft)
SEATING: First class: Second class:	340 51 289
POWER EQUIPMENT: System:	GTO Thyristor ac-dc-3ph ac
TRACTION MOTORS: Rating:	4 815 kW – 3 phase asynchronous
MAX PERMITTED SPEED: Service speed:	210 km/hr (130 mph) 200 km/hr (125 mph)
BRAKING SYSTEM:	Electropneumatic and regenerative

AUTOMATED RAILWAYS

*A*utomation of railway operation is a feature of signalling systems, and such systems were installed on main lines as long ago as the first decade of this century. On underground railways, automatic signalling featured even before that. Today it is commonplace on all forms of rail transport.

Metro systems particularly lend themselves to automated operation. Automatic route-setting has long been a feature of London Underground lines, where track layouts are relatively simple and trains with common characteristics are run to a clear-cut, repetitive pattern. Today on new Rapid Transit lines, computer-based automatic route-setting has been combined with other functions to produce fully-automated systems. In the mid-1950s, the Paris Metro began experimenting with a system designed to regulate the speed of trains over a specially equipped section of line. By the 1960s London Underground was experimenting with a system of automatic train operation (ATO), which was perfected and installed on the Victoria Line in 1968-71.

WITH OR WITHOUT OPERATOR?

So far these systems still employed a train operator to ensure the train was ready to depart and to give a starting signal. From that point the train accelerates, runs, coasts and brakes to a stop at the next station controlled

ABOVE The new cable-stayed bridge over the Fraser River, which carries Vancouver's Skytrain along the 1990 extension to Scott Road, is one of the largest of its kind in the world.

by computer and without any further intervention from the operator.

As long as there are operators and passenger regulation is ad hoc, station stopping times cannot be guaranteed. The ultimate in regularity can be guaranteed only with full automation and 100 per cent reliability, and the latter is rarely achievable. An unmanned fully automatic railway has much in its favour if its users can be persuaded that it is "safe".

The ultimate in automatic train operation is the totally unmanned train, and this was first achieved on the light rapid-transit system in Lille (the VAL system – *Véhicle Automatique Légère* – which opened in 1983) and in the Port Island system in Kobe, Japan, which began running shortly afterwards. The Kobe system is small by comparison with Lille. Today there are a number of fully automated people-mover systems, mainly specialized ones, for example at Gatwick Airport and Dallas-Fort Worth Airport. The Lille system is of particular interest because it is an urban Metro in its own right. There are two other systems of special interest, both with different approaches – the Vancouver Skytrain and the London Docklands Light Railway.

VAL – THE LILLE METRO

In 1969 Lille New Town – Villeneuve d'Ascq – sought a suitable transport system for a link with the centre of the city of Lille. The town authority, known now as EPALE, commissioned Professor Robert Gabillard of the Scientific & Technical Faculty of Lille University to recommend a modern transport system in keeping with the new development. Professor Gabillard recommended a fully automatic rapid-transit system with vehicles running on rubber tyres for quietness, part elevated, part at ground level and part in tunnels.

When his principles were accepted tenders were issued, and Matra's VAL system was chosen. Professor Gabillard and his team of academics and students acted as consultants. Matra Transport, who are signalling and automatic train control specialists, headed a group comprising its own automation company, Interlec; CIMT Lorraine as rolling stock builder; and TCO (Traction-CEM-Oerlikon) to supply the traction equipment (the two latter companies are now incorporated in GEC Alsthom).

The length of the first line was 9 km (5.6 miles) and it was inaugurated on 25 April 1983 when President Mitterand visited Lille and the surrounding area. Public service commenced on 16 May 1983. There were 13 stations on Line 1 and the first, Quatre Cantons, is in the

OPPOSITE Two axles with rubber-tyred wheels carry the pair of permanently coupled car bodies. Each pivoting axle is equipped with steel runners which come into use at switching points.

BELOW The VAL System – *Véhicule Automatique Légère* – opened in Lille, France, in 1983 and is the first totally unmanned train. A similar rapid-transit system was developed shortly after in Kobe, Japan.

OPPOSITE BELOW The train, moving along parallel concrete runways, is guided by horizontal wheels which press against lateral guide rails. The latter also conduct the electricity.

70

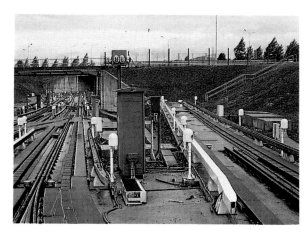

new town of Villeneuve d'Ascq, where the depot is also located. Because trains and stations are normally unmanned, each station has continuous glass panelling along the platform edge with automatic sliding doors which remain closed until a train has come to a standstill. The doors are opened simultaneously with those on the train. Trains are halted within an error of no more than 300 mm (11¾ in).

The basic VAL vehicle is a pair of permanently coupled car bodies, each carried on two axles with rubber-tyred wheels. Each two-car set is 26.14 m (86 ft) long and 2.06 m (6 ft 9 in) wide. There are three Metro systems outside Paris and all operate rubber-tyred trains. The two earlier Metros in Lyons and Marseilles use the system developed by the Paris Metro with bogie vehicles. The Lille vehicles are therefore much smaller and they do not have the steel guide rails of the other two systems. Instead the single axles are equipped with steel runners which only have a function at switching points. Each axle is driven by its own 120kW motor mounted on the vehicle frame, and the drive is through a Cardan shaft. Each axle is free to pivot by a controlled amount.

The track for the carrying wheels is novel and consists of two concrete runways spaced 1.6 m (5 ft 3 in) apart. Guidance is provided by horizontal wheels which press against lateral guide rails, which also act as the positive and negative conductor rails supplying 750V dc to the vehicles. At switches, where there has to be a break in

71

A MATTER OF TIMING ||||

When a train stops at a station platform there is a delay of 1 second, during which time all conditions are checked for safety. If all is correct the train then gives a command to open the doors. Immediately a countdown begins, and after 14 seconds a start command is given by the station. An audible warning sounds, the doors are closed, and after a further series of checks the train departs and accelerates on its way. At busy times the station stop time is increased to 30 seconds, but the procedure remains the same. At the terminal stations trains make the normal station stop and are then run forward into a shunting neck. If all conditions are correct and the other platform is vacant, the points are switched and the train moves into the platform to take on passengers.

EXTENSIONS

An extension 4.4 km (2.75 miles) long was opened in 1984. It has a further five stations and runs due south of the city to the Loos district. Following the success of the first line, a further 11.6 km (7.2 miles) were added with a further 18 stations in 1989. This line, known as Line 1 Bis runs from the main line station southwards through the commercial centre, then turns west to an interchange with Line 1 at Porte des Postes, and then north-west to the Lomme district at St Philibert, where there is an additional depot.

Two more lines are planned and expected to be in operation by 1996. At Gares, the main line railway station, there is also an interchange with a light railway (former tramway) to Roubaix and Tourcoing, popularly known as Le Mongy. This line, which is of conventional type, is, like the VAL system, owned by the Transports en Commun de la Communauté Urbaine de Lille (TCC). It is currently being upgraded and routed to serve the new TGV Nord station.

At present, services are provided by 83 two-car trains. So popular is the VAL system that some 43.5 million passengers are carried annually. VAL systems are also being adopted or proposed for Starboard, Bordeaux (approved for 1996 opening), Rennes (approved in 1989) and Toulouse (10 km of initial route approved in 1985 for opening 1993), while other French provincial cities are said to be interested.

THE LILLE TRANSPORT SYSTEM ||||

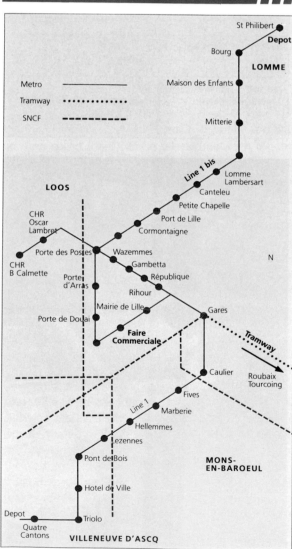

OPPOSITE **The trains, which have a maximum capacity of 208 passengers, can carry some 10,000 people per hour in each direction. Wheelchair access is straightforward, as platforms are flush with train doors, and vertical handrails are positioned by the doors for standing passengers.**

SKYTRAIN – VANCOUVER METRO

A Canadian company, Urban Transportation Development Corporation (UTDC) – founded and originally owned by the Ontario Government – was developing an Intermediate Capacity Transit System (ICTS) designed to cater for up to 25,000 passengers per hour in each direction. Its principal features included: fully automatic operation of lightweight vehicles working singly or, in married pairs, up to six-car trains; steel wheeled steerable bogies running on continuously welded rail (CWR) (see page 81); linear induction motor (LIM) propulsion and regenerative braking (see page 80); slender concrete elevated guideways; and 600V dc power supply. Other features were quietness in operation, low acquisition costs, low operation and maintenance costs, traction independent of friction between wheel and rail, and the ability to negotiate sharp curves. Curves as sharp as 30 m (100 feet) radius are a feature. This was branded as Advanced Light Rapid Transit (ALRT). It is an interesting meld of metro, LRT and people-mover technology.

The first fully operational installation was a Metro feeder system, the Scarborough Line in Toronto, opened in 1985. A second line, the Toronto Harbourfront Line, opened in 1990, making a total of 9 km (6 miles).

BELOW **The lightness of the Skytrain vehicles (14 tons per car) means that they can cope with curves down to 70 metres (230 feet) and 6 per cent gradients.**

75

The two four-level stations on the underground section have multiple escalators and lifts. The tunnel section is 1.6 km (1 mile) long and a further 13 km are of elevated construction. The elevated sections are on lightweight, pre-stressed concrete guideways which carry normal continuously welded rails at standard 1435 mm (4 ft 8½ in) gauge. Ground level (grade) sections are on a reserved guideway. Station platforms are 80 m (265 feet) long and over 30,000 passengers can be handled in one direction. The number of passengers handled per hour is about 8000.

TECHNICAL FEATURES

114 cars were built by UTDC. These are small by Metro standards, being 12.7 m (41 ft 9 in) long, 2.5 m (8 ft 2¾ in) wide and 3.1 m (10 ft 2¼ in) high, with twin double-sliding doors each side. Weighing only 14 tonnes (30,800 lb) empty, they are built of aluminium alloy and can carry 40 seated passengers and a normal standing complement of 35, increasing to 68 under crush conditions. There is also space for two wheelchairs. Track and stations have been designed to permit the introduction of longer and heavier vehicles in the future.

The Seltrac automatic train control system was provided by SEL Canada (a division of ITT) using a system developed for the Berlin U-Bahn. Typically trains are separated by time, of the order of 25 seconds, rather than distance. Allowing for station stop times, the closest sustainable headway is 75 seconds; 60-second headways can be operated but without repeatable regularity.

Whereas the VAL system employs conventional dc motors for propulsion, the ICTS is propelled and braked by a linear induction motor (see below for the definition of a Linear Induction Motor – LIM). Direct current at 600 volts is collected from two side-conductor rails – one above the other – and is converted to alternating current at variable voltage and frequency on the cars, each car having an electronic inverter which handles both power and regenerative braking. Electromagnetic track brakes of German origin are also provided. The trains have hydraulic disc-brakes, manufactured by American companies, for parking.

Like the VAL system, the trains are computer-controlled and nominally unmanned, although to discourage vandals there are roving staff, known as rapid transit attendants (RTAs). These people are trained in public information, first aid, manual driving and can handle minor technical problems such as sticking doors. They also have security, supervisory and ticket-checking responsibilities. The first train each day, while driven automatically, carries an RTA in the front vestibule ready to make an emergency manual stop in case of vandalism or if any object has fallen on the track during the three-hour shut-down period. Tickets are issued from automatic machines and must be carried and produced on demand as proof of payment.

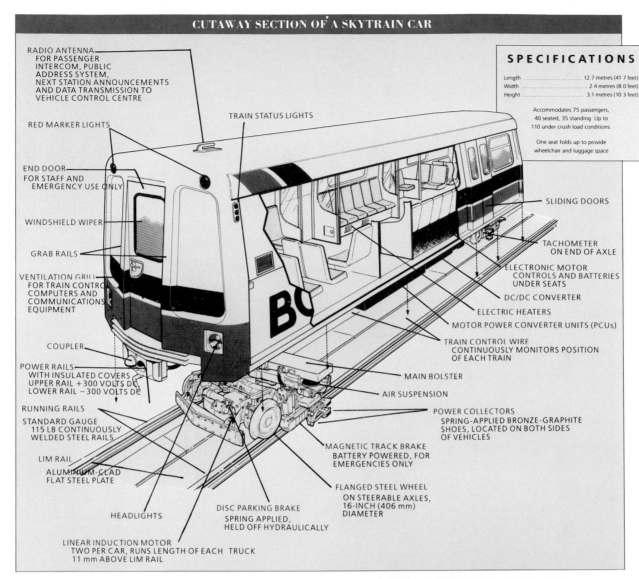

CUTAWAY SECTION OF A SKYTRAIN CAR

RADIO ANTENNA
FOR PASSENGER
INTERCOM, PUBLIC
ADDRESS SYSTEM,
NEXT STATION ANNOUNCEMENTS
AND DATA TRANSMISSION TO
VEHICLE CONTROL CENTRE

TRAIN STATUS LIGHTS

RED MARKER LIGHTS

END DOOR
FOR STAFF AND
EMERGENCY USE ONLY

WINDSHIELD WIPER

GRAB RAILS

VENTILATION GRILL
FOR TRAIN CONTROL
COMPUTERS AND
COMMUNICATIONS
EQUIPMENT

COUPLER

POWER RAILS
WITH INSULATED COVERS
UPPER RAIL +300 VOLTS DC
LOWER RAIL −300 VOLTS DC

RUNNING RAILS

STANDARD GAUGE
115 LB CONTINUOUSLY
WELDED STEEL RAILS

LIM RAIL
ALUMINIUM-CLAD
FLAT STEEL PLATE

HEADLIGHTS

DISC PARKING BRAKE
SPRING APPLIED,
HELD OFF HYDRAULICALLY

LINEAR INDUCTION MOTOR
TWO PER CAR, RUNS LENGTH OF EACH TRUCK
11 mm ABOVE LIM RAIL

SLIDING DOORS

TACHOMETER
ON END OF AXLE

ELECTRONIC MOTOR
CONTROLS AND BATTERIES
UNDER SEATS

DC/DC CONVERTER

ELECTRIC HEATERS

MOTOR POWER CONVERTER UNITS (PCUs)

TRAIN CONTROL WIRE
CONTINUOUSLY MONITORS POSITION
OF EACH TRAIN

MAIN BOLSTER

AIR SUSPENSION

POWER COLLECTORS
SPRING-APPLIED BRONZE-GRAPHITE
SHOES, LOCATED ON BOTH SIDES
OF VEHICLES

MAGNETIC TRACK BRAKE
BATTERY POWERED, FOR
EMERGENCIES ONLY

FLANGED STEEL WHEEL
ON STEERABLE AXLES,
16-INCH (406 mm)
DIAMETER

SPECIFICATIONS

Length	12.7 metres (41 7 feet)
Width	2 4 metres (8 0 feet)
Height	3.1 metres (10 3 feet)

Accommodates 75 passengers,
40 seated, 35 standing Up to
110 under crush load conditions.

One seat folds up to provide
wheelchair and luggage space

79

RIGHT The control centre, which flanks the main line in Burnaby, is responsible for directing train movement and ensuring safe spacing between trains. It also controls the movement of switches and enforces track closures and speed restrictions.

An electric motor works on magnetic attraction and repulsion. In an induction motor, the passage of an alternating current through a specially designed winding on its frame (stator) induces a reaction in another winding on the rotor, which is not electrically connected to the stator. If the stator winding is opened out flat and placed very close to a metal plate, usually of steel or aluminium, the plate will move in the same direction as the stator. If the plate is fixed and the stator winding attached to a wheeled vehicle, the vehicle will move instead.

This is the very broad principle of the linear induction motor.

Its advantage is that movement of a vehicle does not rely on the friction between the wheel treads and the surface on which they are running. The disadvantage is that the motor is more difficult to control, or was before the introduction of modern electronics. Its other advantage in railway traction is its ability to absorb power and act as a brake, generating power as it does so which can be returned to the supply; this is termed regenerative braking.

SKYTRAIN (Vancouver, Canada)	
SYSTEM:	Fully-automated linear-motor driven
Type:	Advanced Light Rapid Transit (ALRT)
Gauge:	1435 mm (4ft 8 in)
Electrical system:	600V dc side rail collection
TRAIN FORMATION:	2-car units
Number of axles:	2×2-axle bogies per car
BUILT:	1985–
Builder:	Metro Canada (UTDC)
Number built:	114 cars
DIMENSIONS:	25.4 m (83 ft 4 in)
Length of car:	12.7 m (41 ft 8 in)
Width:	2.5 m (8 ft 2½ in)
Height:	3.1 m (10 ft 2 in)
Weight:	14 tonnes (13.75 tons)
CAPACITY:	216 per 2-car unit
Seated:	80
Standing – normal:	35
– crush-loaded:	68
Headway:	75 seconds, normal
	60 seconds, minimum irregular
POWER EQUIPMENT:	Inverted dc, variable frequency
System:	Automatic driving
CONTROL SYSTEM:	Central computer controlled
Operating speed:	80 km/hr (50 mph)
TRACTION MOTORS:	Linear induction motor
Number:	1 per car
BRAKING SYSTEM:	LIM regenerative and magnetic track brakes
Operative speeds:	Regenerative to 0 km/hr

CONVENTIONAL ROTARY INDUCTION MOTOR

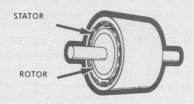

STATOR

ROTOR

LINEAR INDUCTION MOTOR (LIM)

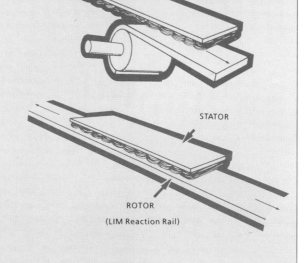

STATOR

ROTOR

(LIM Reaction Rail)

STEERING AXLE BOGIE

Usually railway coaches run on bogies in which the axles are connected to the frames through "elastic" systems in fixed positions parallel to each other. Axle spacing is usually around 2000-2750 mm (7-9 ft). On very sharp curves, the wheel flanges contact the rails at an angle, and not only do they wear each other but they also produce a lot of unpleasant noise and vibration. If the axles are allowed some freedom this wear and noise is reduced, but safety at speed is also reduced. By interconnecting the axles through two "elastic" systems, the axles can be angled on curves and the bogie "steers" through them with less wear and noise. Less wear on flanges and rails occurs at the expense of a more complicated suspension system, with more joints in the bogie mechanism.

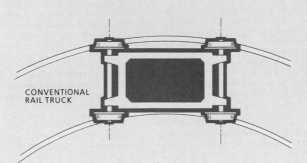

CONVENTIONAL
RAIL TRUCK

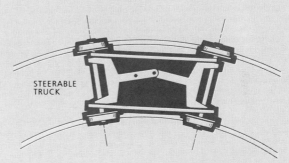

STEERABLE
TRUCK

81

DOCKLANDS LIGHT RAILWAY (DLR)

Like the two previous systems, the London Docklands Light Railway (DLR) was developed without many of the constraints that apply to long-established rail systems. It did have a few of its own, not least of which were severely restricted finance and a short time scale. One particular problem was the need to satisfy no fewer than three major bodies: the London Docklands Development Corporation (LDDC), the Greater London Council (GLC) and the British Government.

DLR was authorized in 1982 as a major infrastructure investment aimed at attracting industry to the former dockside areas of East London. Several proposals were examined – some involving considerable tunnelling were rejected on the grounds of cost – and most included street running. It was expected that the eventual system would employ some version of the classic European three-bogie streetcar. By mid-1983 the route had crystallized to one of total segregation with no tunnels. The need to minimize the use of land together with the ability of lightweight rail to operate with steep gradients and sharp curves led ultimately to a route which made use of both of these factors and the disused trackbeds of former main-line routes.

BIDDING TO BUILD

With a maximum projected flow of only 1500 passengers per hour between the City and the Isle of Dogs, DLR was at the lower end of the light rail spectrum. In 1984 the British Government showed a preference for an all-embracing "design and construct" contract for the whole railway. Within that constraint, five consortia tendered for the contract, proposing fairly conventional 2.65 m (8ft 9 in) wide six-axle light rail vehicles. UTDC offered married pairs of four-axle cars, and Matra the complete VAL package with rubber-tyred cars. The latter suffered

BELOW A designer's prototype of a DLR vehicle at a station platform is inset into an artist's impression of the completed North Quay junction.

OPPOSITE The Docklands development scheme was the flagship of Mrs Thatcher's Government, and was intended to attract industry to East London's once bustling dockside areas. The light railway was an important element in attracting a sizeable workforce into the area.

82

some cost disadvantage because the trackway could not benefit from the use of existing disused trackbeds, and stations would have to have trackside screens and doors.

Eventually, from a short-list of two, the contract was awarded to the GEC-Mowlem Railway group. During the contract discussions three major decisions were taken in order to get the best passenger facilities from the very limited sum of money available:

1. trains would be automatically driven;

2. current collection would be from a third rail to avoid unsightly catenary wires (this was at the request of the LDDC);

3. full access would be provided for wheelchair passengers.

ROUTE

The final route begins at an elevated station close to the Tower of London, to be called Tower Gateway, and runs alongside the British Rail London-Southend line from Fenchurch Street. It then passes across an old viaduct of the former London and Blackwall Railway from Stepney Junction towards Poplar. There the line to the Isle of Dogs sweeps sharply to the south on elevated structures across the old dock basins to a station close to the river at Island Gardens (North Greenwich). A triangular junction takes the route east for a short distance then north to Stratford, partly on the trackbed of the former North London Railway, where there is cross-platform interchange with British Railways. Trains run typically from Tower Gateway to Island Gardens and then to Stratford and vice versa.

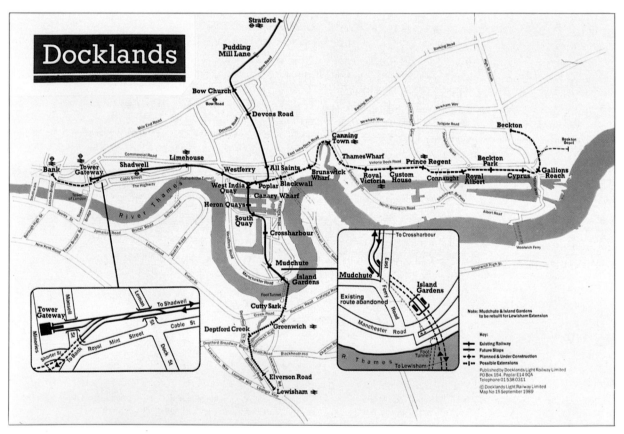

CARS AND STAFF

Cars 28 m (92 ft 1½ in) long were proposed by GEC-Mowlem and accepted. The 11 cars have two half-bodies mounted on three bogies, and the stated carrying capacity is 227 people. Each half-body has two double inward-opening plug doors, and the seating layout is a mixture of transverse and longitudinal bays. As there is normally no driver, there are forward-facing seats that give a wide view of the track ahead and behind.

The cars are based on the European three-bogie light-rail vehicles, and because there was no experience with

that type of vehicle in Britain the order to build them went to Linke-Hofmann-Busch at Salzgitter in Germany. The GEC and LDDC had strong, if not always similar, views as to what was wanted and the manufacturer did well to produce a reasonable-looking vehicle which has been proved to be on the right lines with seat design, windows, general finish and lighting.

An attendant – known as a Train Captain – is carried. It is his or her duty to check tickets, help disabled passengers on and off, keep a general eye on things and finally to act as dispatcher, closing the doors and giving

SPECIAL FEATURES OF DLR CARS

The new cars will have the following features:

sliding doors

longitudinal seats between the doors of each
    half-body

passenger standing areas in doorways

external "car fault" indicators

fault diagnosis and annunciator equipment

ability to operate in three-car rakes in normal
    service and as six cars in emergency

relocated train dispatch controls

Category I fire rating

BELOW This indicates the position taken up by the driver if there is a breakdown of the automatic system. The fault indicator panel is to the right of the emergency door.

BELOW Construction of the DLR track in progress at Canary Wharf, London, in 1990.

85

the starting signal to the control computer. In an emergency he or she may also drive the train from a set of driving controls in the normal position at the front of the vehicle. Normally the Train Captain takes up a position at one of the inner doors.

LATER DEVELOPMENTS

DLR was opened by Queen Elizabeth II in 1987 and immediately became popular. Traffic forecasts were totally wrong from the beginning as was shown by the 50,000 passengers carried on the first public holiday of 31 August 1987 — twice the level of passengers forecast for the railway in its stable post-1992 state! Not only that but a forecast of 3500 jobs on Canary Wharf had grown first to 40,000 then 60,000. To cope with this deluge the railway had to grow fast.

Even before DLR opened a necessary extension in tunnel to the Bank (Bank of England in the City of London) had been authorized. Not only that but the pessimistic traffic forecasts had been exceeded within the first year of operation, and it was clear that an upgrading was

necessary. GEC-Mowlem were given the upgrading contract to lengthen stations to take two-car trains and to build a further batch of vehicles. The short time-scale inhibited the chance of making any significant changes. In particular the unsatisfactory passenger doors had to be perpetuated. The additional cars were built to Linke-Hofmann-Busch licence by BREL.

Because of developments of London's docklands, the railway is being extended eastwards to Beckton and possibly even as far as Barking. There is also a proposal for a southwards extension under the River Thames through a tunnel and on to Lewisham. Work on the Beckton extension is under way, and new rolling stock has been ordered from a Belgian-British consortium.

DLR was originally conceived mostly as a showpiece and quiet light railway — something to which a government with little concern for public transport gave lip service. Now DLR is having to adapt and will become more of a light Metro. The cars will have to change into ones suited to a mass carrier without any significant loss of passenger appeal.

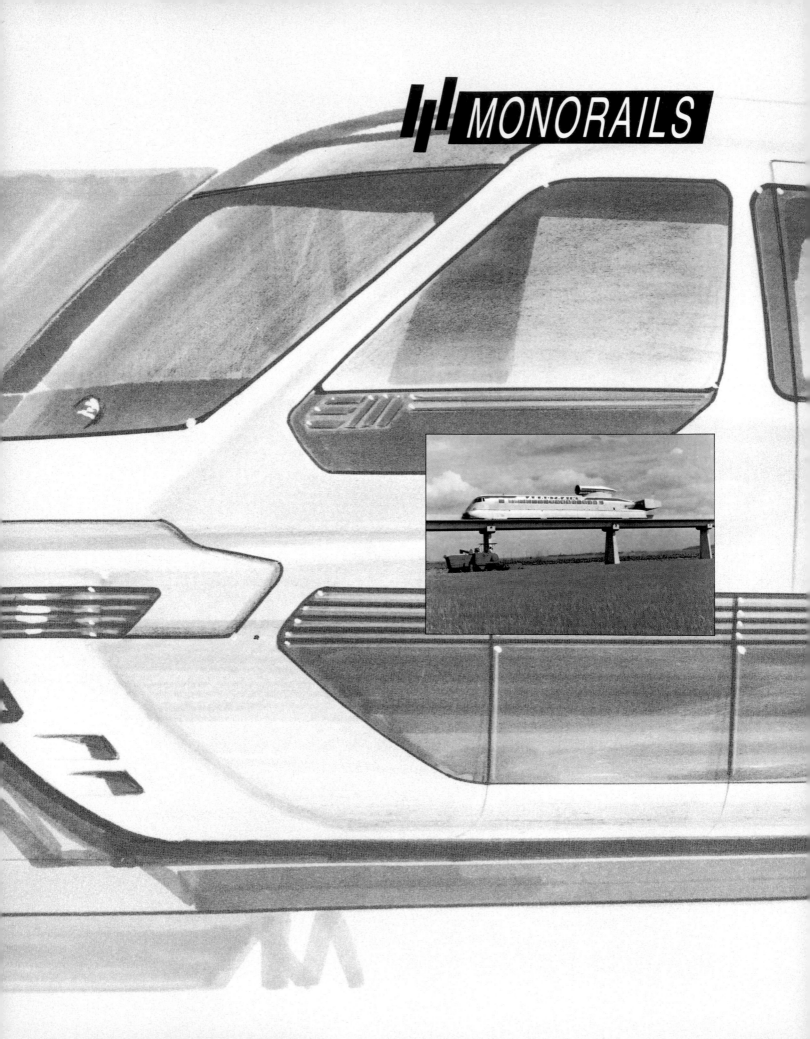

The very word *monorail* conjures up a picture of some futuristic transport system such as that probably in H. G. Wells' mind when he wrote *The Shape of Things to Come*. But what do we mean by a monorail? Literally it is a transport system employing a single rail. But why monorails? Ideally, a single rail offers less resistance to motion, particularly on curves, and should be "self guiding". But supporting a vehicle on a single rail needs delicate balance or the assistance of a gyroscope to provide equilibrium. From the middle of the 19th century, several engineers have pondered on the problem of designing monorails. Even today they are something of a rarity.

So-called monorails come in two forms – suspended and supported. They are normally employed in special locations and are cost effective mainly where conventional railway construction is difficult or there is some other appeal – for example in theme parks. The accompanying drawing illustrates different types of elevated construction. Because of the stability problems, the true monorail ideal remained dormant for a long while. On the other hand suspended railways which use a single rail or cable have thrived and it is only in the last two or three decades that supported monorails have found favour in a number of special cases.

DIFFERENT TYPES OF ELEVATED CONSTRUCTION

SUPPORTED MONORAIL

TRACK GUIDED TRAINWAY

ASYMMETRICALLY SUSPENDED MONORAIL

SYMMETRICALLY SUSPENDED MONORAIL

SUPPORTED MONORAILS

In modern times, the main uses of supported monorails have been for urban transport (for which overhead construction is necessary) and in scenic locations. This has arisen mainly from the need to provide an easy right-of-way. A monorail system which is carried overhead in a city may revert to ground level or even go underground where conditions permit, as when serving an airport.

Monorails do not have a monopoly of overhead transport, as can be seen in many cities in the United States in particular, where many miles of motorway viaduct and flyovers are a considerable intrusion. Also there are many miles of elevated conventional railways and more may well be built in the future. A generation which is quite prepared to tolerate concrete viaducts and flyovers above its back yards may well come round again to tolerating overhead railways, particularly as today noise levels have become much lower.

In the early 1960s, plans were being made for a high-speed rail link from London (Victoria Station) to the airport at Heathrow. Hearing of plans by Tokyo and other

RIGHT **Sydney's Darling Harbour monorail, so far the only example of its kind in Australia, is 3.6 km (2.3 miles) long and employs six train sets of the type shown.**

cities for monorails, a Parliamentary pressure-group proposed an alternative and "thoroughly modern" monorail scheme. The main-line rail scheme was dropped and deeper investigation of the monorail proposal showed that the sums had not been done properly and it was not viable. The main-line rail connection to London Heathrow is only now being built!

Most of today's monorails run on concrete guideways and have rubber-tyred vehicles. The system that has found the widest use is the Alweg, a German development first demonstrated in Cologne in 1956-7 on a single line of about 1.6 km (1 mile) in length. The accompanying drawing shows the arrangement of the driving, guiding and stabilizing wheels from which it can be seen that the system is by no means as simple as the term Monorail might be thought to imply. It was adopted for Disney-land in the USA in 1959 and, later, 1961. There the trains run on elevated structures well above the parks them-selves and provide riders with a panoramic view of the whole area.

In Japan a number of cities have adopted either straddle or suspended monorails for relatively short lines. Chiba and Shonan have suspended systems totalling 22 km (13.7 miles). Kitakyushu (8.4 km/5¼ miles), Nagoya (1.2 km/¾ mile), Odakyu (1.1 km/¾ mile) and Tokyo have straddle systems – the latter being 13.2 km (8.2 miles) long, linking Tokyo's inner city with the Haneda airport; it is probably the best known.

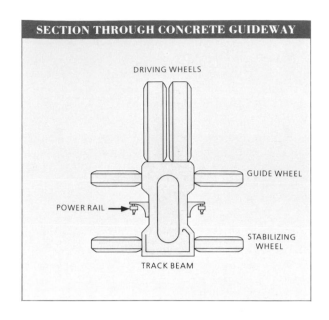

SECTION THROUGH CONCRETE GUIDEWAY

DRIVING WHEELS

GUIDE WHEEL

POWER RAIL →

STABILIZING WHEEL

TRACK BEAM

BELOW Shot of Germany's Transrapid 06 on the test track at Cologne. This experimental set-up managed to reach some very high speeds and was, before safety problems flared up, a serious contender for one of the high-speed intercity routes.

AN EARLY EXPERIMENT

A monorail was built as long ago as the early 1880s, the invention of a Frenchman, Charles Lartigue. Legend has it that the inventor stood one day in the Algerian desert watching the passage of a camel train. Intrigued by the delicately-balanced panniers carried by the animals, he conceived a transport system with the loads balanced on either side of a single central rail. He therefore set out to build a practical monorail.

He staged a demonstration in Brussels, then built a line between Feurs and Panissières in France. On 29 February 1888, a 15.3 km (9½ mile) line opened in the west of Ireland between Listowel and Ballybunnion. While the French line had a very short life, the L & B lasted 36 years and was finally closed on 14 October 1924 after having been severely damaged during the Irish Civil War. Being unique, the little railway was reasonably well patronized although mainly by summer visitors. World War I and the subsequent increase in road traffic finally took their toll and the company could not survive the traffic lost through the war damage.

Although nominally a "mono-rail", it actually employed three rails, one on the topside of a triangular trestle, and two horizontal guide rails for stability. There were three steam locomotives, each with two boilers – one each side of the centre rail. Carriages and wagons were also double. One of the operating problems, particularly when carrying freight, was the need to balance the loads, and if a cow was to be carried from one end of the line to the other, two calves of an equivalent weight had to be carried out and back again!

In 1910 Louis Brennan demonstrated a pure monorail in London. Motor cars balanced by large gyroscopes ran with double-flanged wheels on one ordinary steel rail laid on the ground. Such was the initial enthusiasm with which it was received that many predicted it was the end of the conventional railway. Somehow the enthusiasm died.

89

LEFT AND BELOW In 1910, the Brennan monorail underwent tests at Gillingham, England. By adapting a gyroscope with two wheels revolving in opposite directions in a vacuum, a 22-ton car could be driven at considerable speed along the 600 m (1,970 feet) curved track.

TOKYO AIRPORT MONORAIL

When it was opened in 1964, the Tokyo airport monorail looked like being a white elephant and had to be sponsored. Then, following increased traffic congestion and an improved interchange with the Metro and buses at the inner city terminal, more people began to use the Hamamatsu-cho, although even now the peak of 6000 passengers an hour in one direction only just makes it worthwhile. Today Haneda airport handles only domestic flights, and a 6.1 km (3.8 mile) extension is under construction from Haneda-Seibijo to the new international airport at Higashi-Kuko, due to open in 1993, when the section from Haneda-Seibijo to Haneda will be closed.

The line is built on the Alweg system by Hitachi and there are three intermediate stations. The two-track airport terminal station was built under the plaza in front of the airport building. The route then passes in a single-track tunnel under one runway, and after 742 m (814 yards) in a tunnel runs at ground level to leave the airport area, where it becomes double-track. It then enters a double-track 448 m (491 yards) tunnel under the Ebitori river, and emerges to run over the sea for a distance of

CUTAWAY SECTION OF TOKYO AIRPORT MONORAIL

90

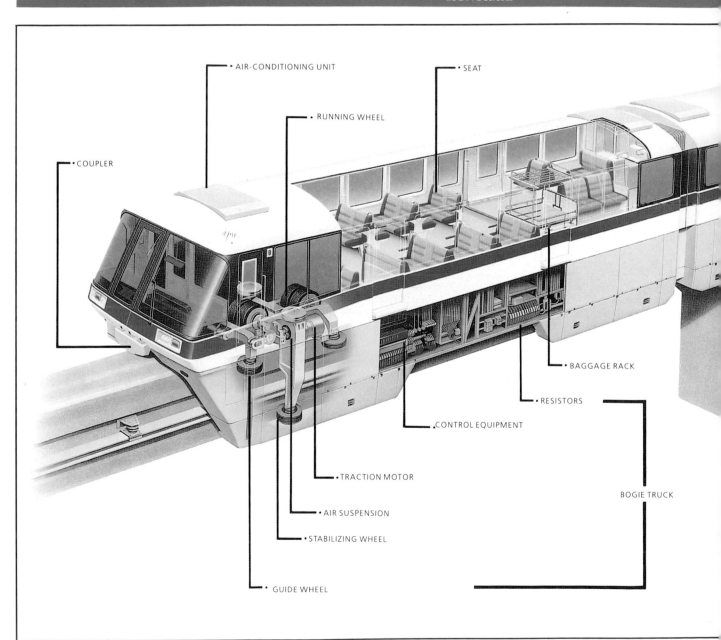

- AIR-CONDITIONING UNIT
- SEAT
- RUNNING WHEEL
- COUPLER
- BAGGAGE RACK
- RESISTORS
- CONTROL EQUIPMENT
- TRACTION MOTOR
- BOGIE TRUCK
- AIR SUSPENSION
- STABILIZING WHEEL
- GUIDE WHEEL

8974 m (5.6 miles) supported on piles built on the sea bed of Tokyo Bay. From there it runs overland on elevated concrete structures, crossing the main highway, a canal and main-line railway to reach the city terminal at Hamamatsu-cho. This is about one mile from the central main-line railway station. Three intermediate stations serve commercial developments.

Nearly all the tracks are concrete beams, with a few steel beams in special locations. A single beam is provided for each direction of travel, which justifies the name monorail. But there the similarity to a railway ceases. The vehicles are carried on undercarriages, each of which has four rubber-tyred driving wheels running on the top of the beam. Guidance is by six more pairs of rubber-tyred wheels that run against the vertical sides of the beam. To keep the total height of the vehicles reasonable, the tops of the driving wheels are above the floor level. Where this occurs, the seating is arranged back-to-back down the centre of the car, with a consequent loss of seating capacity. There are 72 cars, all motorized.

Propulsion is by electricity at 750 volts dc. The positive and negative conductor rails are located on each side of the beam's vertical walls. The car sheds and maintenance depot are situated at Showajima, 3.1 km (1.9 miles) from the Haneda terminal. Because of the difficulty of installing crossovers, trains can enter and leave the depot only from the track nearest to it.

When the line was built, it was claimed that it was designed for a maximum speed of 100 km/h (62 mph), although the timetables were originally based on a maximum speed of 80 km/h (50 mph). It is doubtful if this figure is attained in regular service. Trains, manually driven, run at approximately 6 minute intervals, and up to nine cars can be run in peak times. The maximum gradient is 6 per cent (1 in 16.7), while the minimum radius of curve that can be negotiated (at low speed) is 120 m (395 feet).

Fixed signalling is provided, and the system checks in and checks out the progress of each train from one block section to another. A cab-signalling system supplements the fixed signals, and there is an automatic train-stop device interlocked with the signals. Radio and telephone communication with the "ground" is also provided.

Snow and ice, although relatively infrequent in Tokyo, can present winter operating problems. A snow sweeper is used, consisting of a vehicle with rotating brushes which is pushed along the guideways by a special pusher powered by an internal combustion engine.

An even longer monorail is now under construction in Tokyo. A new north-south line 16 km long, known as the Tama Urban Monorail, will run from Tama New Town in Tokyo's western suburbs. It will link Tama Centre with Tachikawa and Kamikitadai to provide connections with several radial conventional rail routes into central Tokyo. The first 5.4 km (3.4 miles) of the new line are due to open in 1992, the remainder in 1997.

91

BELOW The Tokyo Airport monorail is the world's first fully operational straddle-type monorail system; since September 1964, it has transported more than 600 million passengers.

THE SCHWEBEBAHN AND SUSPENDED MONORAILS

Probably the most famous suspended railway is in the Wuppertal, Germany – the Schwebebahn. This Langen system line was opened in 1901, is 13.3 km (8¼ miles) long with 19 stations, and runs from Oberbarmen, through Elberfeld to Vohwinkel, near Essen, following the river Wupper. The Wupper valley is fairly steep-sided and road building was rather difficult, so a monorail had a special attraction. The twin "tracks" are supported about every 200-300 m (660-990 ft) from A-shaped and inverted U-shaped steel structures. For most of the length the line is carried above the river and in some places over the streets. To avoid complicated switches, loops with a radius of only 9 m (30 ft) are provided at the terminals.

Two-car trains are run, the supporting structures are not strong enough for longer trains. In peak periods trains can be run to a headway of 2½ minutes, while at off-peak times the interval between trains is about 10 minutes. The original trains, which had wooden bodies and carried 50 passengers, weighed about 12 tonnes (26,880 lb) and were 11.25 m (37 ft) long. These have been replaced by 28 new lightweight metal cars of about the same length but slightly wider which carry 60 passengers. In peak hours the "crush-loading" can exceed 100 passengers per car.

For a line built in 1901 a maximum permitted speed of 60 km/h (37 mph) was quite ambitious, but in normal service it is rare for the speed to exceed 40 km/h (25 mph). The normal journey time for a train stopping at all stations is 35 minutes – an average speed of 22.8 km/h (14 mph). The maximum gradient is 2.7 per cent (1 in 37). Propulsion is provided by two 60hp electric motors on each car fed from a 600V dc system. Compressed-air braking is used.

In spite of the fact that the structures and rails are of steel, noise is acceptable both inside the vehicles and in the street. The riding of the vehicles is also very good.

RIGHT The Schwebebahn suspended railway takes 35 minutes to complete its run of 13.3 km (8.2 miles), which includes stopping at 17 stations. The rails are supported by 472 girders, and a total of 19,200 tons of iron were used to build the framework.

OPPOSITE The French Aéro-train was a doomed attempt to adapt the monorail by using air cushions as a means of suspension. Problems with noise and current collection at high speeds scuppered the project at the test stage.

THE FUTURE OF MONORAILS

As long ago as 1966, a convention was arranged by the Railway Engineering Group of the British Institution of Mechanical Engineers in London to consider all aspects of "Guided Land Transport". The following comment was made about the future of monorails:

> It seems unlikely that they [monorails] will develop as a form of super high-speed inter-urban transport . . . Their natural field is clearly for overhead transport in circumstances where right of way problems make a surface line too difficult, as is the case now in almost any city. Thus they seem likely to be applied to carry people between city centres and suburban homes or adjacent airports, and for similar cases

. . . It seems likely that the monorail has some amenity advantage in that the beams are comparatively narrow and therefore the sky is less obscured.

None of this has really changed in the intervening years. Those systems developed since – and there have been very few of them – are either in existence for the reasons stated or for their novelty value. The advantages of a monorail over an orthodox railway of either light or heavy construction are rather less apparent than its enthusiastic protagonists would like us to believe. It is relatively inelastic, it has switching and junction problems which are considerable, and in most cases comparison with an orthodox railway

where a reasonably high traffic density would appear to justify their construction.
The monorail [is left] as a competitor to a two-rail railway, the latter taking a more or less conventional form. In this connection it should therefore be noted that monorails have been essentially developed as an overhead system, and that running on the level or in tunnels is achieved by shortening the supporting pylons down to stubs. By contrast the railway is naturally designed for ground level (or tunnels) and its construction overhead is achieved by what is essentially the technique of the viaduct

shows the latter to be more economical. This has not deterred inventors and others from putting forward more alternatives to the conventional railway, most of which have been abandoned at the testing stage.
Both British Tracked Hovercraft Limited and Bertin & Cie in France conducted experiments in developing air-cushion vehicles. Unfortunately, both systems – the Hovertrain and the Aérotrain – foundered because there were insufficient funds to deal with the problems of suspension, maintaining safety, current collection at high speeds and noise. Both plans were shelved.

93

OTHER SYSTEMS

Today there are still a number of systems being investigated. One, the Eurotren Monoviga EM403, was designed for the link between Madrid and Barajas airport. The line will be 13 km (8 miles) long and is again a single-beam elevated monorail running for the most part 5 m (16 ft 6 in) above ground level, except for the first 3.5 km (2.2 miles), which will use the existing tunnel from Chamartin railway station and the centre of the city. The line is expected to carry 25 million passengers a year.

The inventor of the system, Pinto Silva, is said to have "critically analysed and reevaluated standard railway engineering principles to create new solutions for transport using a guiding track". As a result, he is said to have "drastically broken away from these proven techniques and has moved into new domains". His design is a guided single-beam monorail which is said to have a high-speed capability – 200 km/h (125 mph) for the EM403 which is planned for suburban transport.

A prototype ran on a small elliptical test track in Sevilla from 1987 to June 1989. There, due to curvature of 135 m (444 feet) radius, speed was limited to 135 km/h (64 mph). Vertical carrier wheels and horizontal guide wheels have rubber tyres and provide a secure link between vehicle and track. The two sets of wheels provide complete protection from derailment because of the stabilizing horizontal wheels, which run in wide grooves on the sides of the beams.

The short vehicles are a series of modules 6 m (19 ft 9 in) long constructed from lightweight stainless steel. Each module weighs about 7 tonnes (15,400 lb), and conventional buffers and drawbars are replaced by ball and socket joints. The modules are sealed at the edges by a flexible diaphragm, which leaves the interiors completely clear of dividing walls, rather like the interior of a long flexible tube. A total train set will normally be formed of 12-15 modules.

The carrier wheels form four independently swivelling "rodales" arranged asymmetrically under each module, and propulsion will normally be by three-phase electric motors. It remains to be seen how this new system will perform in service.

"New" ideas are always being promulgated. One of the most promising for very high speeds seemed to be the electro-magnetically supported vehicles known as Maglev. Both the German and Japanese systems seem to have suffered setbacks and still have some way to go. Some of the pioneering experimental work will be discussed in the final chapter.

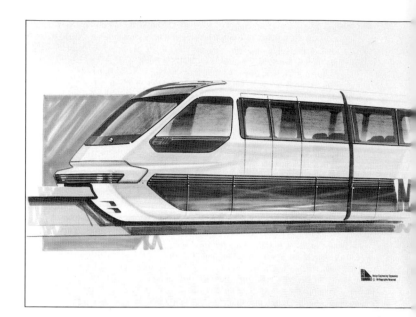

RIGHT **Still at prototype stage, the Eurotren Monoviga is a single-beam monorail designed to connect Madrid and Barajas** **Airport 13 km (8 miles) away. The train will, it is said, be capable of speeds of up to 200 km/h (125 mph).**

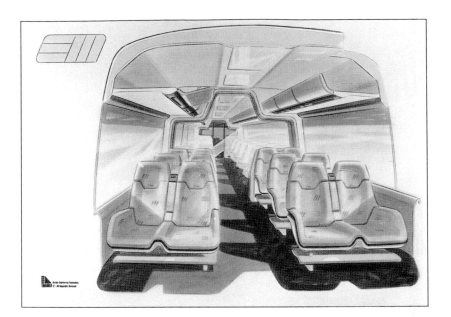

LEFT AND FAR LEFT Early designers' prototypes of the Eurotren Monoviga show how the vehicle interlocks with the 5 m-high (16ft 6in-) concrete guiderail, as well as the passenger seating arrangements.

95

*T*oday the term "heavy haul" conjures up visions of exceptionally long and heavy trains carrying iron ore, coal, phosphates, and so on, on dedicated, privately-owned railways. This is not accepted by a large number of North American Railroads, where it has been the practice for many years to run long and heavy trains of more general merchandise over considerable distances. It must be said, though, that the specialized mineral railways do have their own problems and are of particular interest. Here we shall discuss two of them.

Early railways developed from horse-drawn wagon-ways for the haulage of coal in the north-east of England and in Wales. The Stockton and Darlington Railway was the world's first public railway. Although it carried passengers, it was constructed primarily for the conveyance of coal and coke and, compared to the horse-worked wagonways, in 1825 rated as "heavy haul". In the first nine months of operation with steam traction it carried almost 43,000 tons of coal and coke with 4400 tons of general merchandise.

ECONOMIC CONSIDERATIONS

In the United States and Canada in particular, it is economical to run very long and heavy trains over very difficult terrain. Some of the largest steam locomotives were developed in the United States for just such trains, and there are few followers of railways who do not know of the Big Boys, those huge 772,000 lb (345 ton) 24-wheel monsters of the Union Pacific Railroad. They were built by the American Locomotive Company (Alco) from 1941, primarily for the line between Cheyenne, Wyoming over the 2442 m (8013 ft) Sherman Summit, where a pair would haul 90-100 freight cars with an overall efficiency of no more than 8 per cent at the drawbar. They lasted to the end of steam and one is now preserved.

Individual axle loads of 30-35 tonnes are not unusual on North American railroads, and some even seek to go to 37 tonnes. There is commercial pressure in the United States to go to the "125 (load) ton car" with an axle load of 35.7 tonnes. This worries the Chief Engineers, who are well aware that even with 30-35 tonnes track and bridge repair costs are "rising at an alarming rate".

Today there are a number of lines that have been constructed solely for the purpose of conveying coal, iron ore, phosphates, and so on from mines to coastal ports. Descriptions follow of two of these lines, in South Africa and Australia, the first now electrified and the second with diesel traction. There are others in the United States and Canada but, apart from local differences, the principles are similar.

ABOVE AND BELOW The Minnesota-based Missabe Iron Ranger is one of the few heavy-haul railways specifically dealing in iron ore freight in the US. It is a notable feature of the American scene that more general merchandise is transported in trains with 100 vehicles or more.

SOUTH AFRICAN IRON AND STEEL CORPORATION

The iron ore mines at Sishen in Cape Province are operated by ISCOR (Iron and Steel Corporation). Sishen is over 800 km (500 miles) from the coast, where a specially constructed ore terminal for deep-water vessels has been built at Saldanha. Sishen is some 1300 m (4280 ft) above sea level and the two are joined by 864 km (537 miles) of railway. So that parts of the line could be used by trains of the South African Railways, their gauge of 1067 mm (3 ft 6 in) was chosen. The line runs northwards for 175 km (108 miles) in the coastal region then over the next 200 km (125 miles) climbs to around 950 m (3125 ft), mainly in semi-desert terrain. The remaining 490 km (304 miles) undulate between 800 and 1300 m (2600 and 4300 ft). There is one tunnel and a few bridges, but in the main the line runs through open country.

The terrain traversed is particularly unfriendly. In the coastal region there is frequently salt-laden spray from the ocean; much of the line runs through semi-desert with wind-driven sand. Many severe electrical storms occur, with particularly bad lightning. None of this is particularly attractive to electric traction engineers.

WEIGHT

At first trains of 202 wagons with a gross laden weight of 20,200 tonnes (19,840 tons) were hauled by five diesel-electric locomotives, but it was planned from the beginning that the line would be electrified. The South African Railways are electrified on the 3000V dc system, but it was clear from the outset that it would not be suitable for the ISCOR operation. ISCOR chose a 50kV (rather than 25kV) single-phase ac system as only six feeder stations would be required as opposed to 21 for a 25kV system. The operator would have had to fund the additional feeder stations and transmission lines in a very sparsely populated area.

ISCOR specified the same gross load of 20,200 tonnes (19,840 tons). This meant that to provide sufficient traction for starting such heavy trains, three six-axle locomotives weighing some 168 tonnes (165 tons) with an output around 3780kW (5070hp) would be required. These are large locomotives for a narrow gauge railway. Loaded trains from the mines have to negotiate adverse gradients of 0.4 per cent (1 in 250) along stretches of up to 50 km (31 miles) in length, and it was specified that such gradients must be negotiated at a minimum speed of 34.5 km/h (21.5 mph). Also a train of 20,200 tonnes (19,840 tons) would have to be started on such a gradient and accelerated to the same speed. Down hill the gradients are steeper and even longer stretches of 1 per cent (1 in 100) gradient have to be negotiated with the speed

of the train held at around the same figure. To save mechanical wear and tear, electric "rheostatic" braking is provided, the motors acting as generators. The power produced is dissipated in resistances.

The journeys are of necessity relatively slow and, because the line traverses substantially desert terrain, with tropical temperatures by day and relative cold at night (+45°C to −8°C), comfort for the crews is important. Air-conditioning is provided in the driving cabs, which are some of the largest in use and contain a number of comforts for the crew. An interesting item is a small "garage" on each locomotive, which houses a motorcycle. This is situated between the two bogies, and the motorcycle is used by one crew member who inspects the train. It is also useful in the case of a defect. One has to remember that each train is some 2.3 to 2.5 km (1.4-1.55 miles) in length!

SALDANHA TO SISHEN (South Africa)	
TRAFFIC:	Iron ore
Gauge:	1067 mm (3 ft 6 in)
Length of haul:	846 km (526 miles)
Max train weight:	22880 tonnes (22470 tons)
Locomotives per train:	3
Speed on 0.4% (1 in 250) gradient:	34.5 km/hr (21.5 mph)
TRACTION:	Electric
System:	50kV ac 50 hz
LOCOMOTIVE TYPE:	Co-Co
Weight:	168 tonnes (165 tons)
Number of motors:	6
Continuous rating:	3780 kW
Starting tractive effort:	565 kN (127,160 lb)
Traction motor rating:	670 kW at 1540 volts
Motor type:	Sep. excited, rectified ac
Maximum speed:	90 km/hr (56 mph)
Length, over buffer beams:	20120 mm (66 ft)
Width over body:	2900 mm (9 ft 6 in)
Height of body from rail:	3900 mm (12 ft 9½ in)
Distance between bogie pivots:	127000 mm (41 ft 8 in)
Bogie wheelbase:	3940 mm (12 ft 11 in)
Design:	GEC Traction, Manchester
Locomotive builder:	Union Carriage & Wagon
Electrical equipment:	GEC
Number of locomotives	31

99

LEFT The South African iron ore train, with a gross load of 20,200 tonnes (19,840 tons) and a length of up to 2.5 km (1.5 miles), has to negotiate a windy, semi-desert terrain.

SALDANHA TO SISHEN ROUTE PROFILE

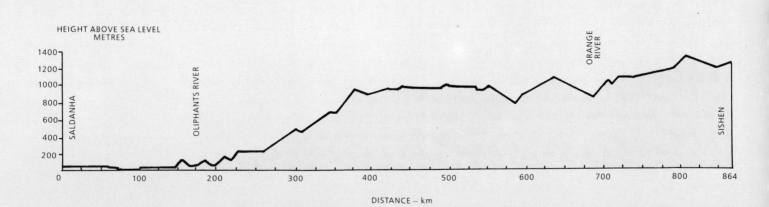

HEIGHT ABOVE SEA LEVEL
METRES

1400
1200
1000
800
600
400
200

SALDANHA
OLIPHANTS RIVER
ORANGE RIVER
SISHEN

0   100   200   300   400   500   600   700   800   864

DISTANCE – km

LOCOMOTIVES AND WAGONS

The locomotives are an unusual shape, with a driving cab at one end only. The opposite end of the locomotive has a lowered roof section which houses the current collector and much of the high-voltage switchgear. This arises because, without passenger traffic and hence platforms, the overhead wire is carried lower than would otherwise be the case, and no screening is needed for the high-voltage roof equipment. This does not mean that passenger vehicles cannot be used, should the need arise, as long as they are of the same dimensions as the raised body and cab portions of the locomotives.

Hi-tech electrical equipment is used. The high voltage of 50kV led to some careful design of some components, notably the main protection equipment, particularly because the line passes through an area where there are many electrical storms. Current is collected from the overhead line by a single pantograph on each locomotive, and fed to a single transformer with an input of 5685kVA. To obtain the best performance, the locomotive has continuously-variable thyristor control. The transformer also provides all auxiliary supplies. Current from the transformer's secondary windings is rectified and fed to the six traction motors.

The original study for the electrification of the line was based on moving some 17.5 million tonnes of ore each year. During the first 18 months of electric operation of the line, some 30 million tonnes of ore were shifted. Train loads were increased from the original 202 100-tonne wagons to 210 wagons of 104 tonnes. Later tests were made with a train of 22,626 tonnes (22,221 tons). As a result, trains were increased to 220 wagons of 104 tonnes. Train lengths have of course also increased from 2.3 km, through 2.4 km to 2.5 km (1.55 miles).

The first order for 25 locomotives was placed by ISCOR. The line has now been taken over by the South African Railways (SAR), and the locomotives have been designated Class 9E. Subsequently six further locomotives were ordered by SAR, and these incorporated a number of changes dictated by SAR specification. The major differences between the two series are in the driving cabs, now in line with SAR standards, and the bogies.

As can be seen the wagons have also undergone some changes and now have a gross weight of 104 tonnes (228,800 lb). The terminals at each end of the lines have been specially designed to minimize the time taken for loading and unloading. Trains are normally formed with three locomotives in such a way that there is a driving cab at each end of the rake. Braking of such long and heavy trains is always difficult, especially where different parts of the train are on different gradients. This is particularly marked with a loaded train, and drivers have to take great care where the gradient changes from up to down and vice versa. The continuously-variable control of power of the locomotives assists the driver in making a smooth change from power to brake and back again.

100

THE HAMERSLEY RAILWAY

The Pilbara district of Western Australia is one of the most remote and inhospitable places in the world, yet it has no fewer than four standard-gauge railways (1435 mm/4 ft 8½ in) built specifically to carry iron ore. These are the Hamersley Railway, the Robe River Railway, the Goldsworthy Railway and the Mount Newman Railway. Probably the best known is the Hamersley.

RIGHT **Each of Hamersley Railway's 47 diesel-electric locomotives is equipped with various hi-tech features suited to local conditions, including air conditioning inside the cabs, extended-range dynamic braking and AAR Type F interlocking couplers.**

HISTORY AND TERRAIN

The Hamersley Railway runs from Dampier on Western Australia's northern coast south across arid country into a mountainous region, rich in iron ore. In 1964 Japan's apparently insatiable appetite for iron ore resulted in an agreement between the Japanese and Hamersley Iron Property Ltd for the purchase of some 65.5 million tonnes (64.3 million tons) of ore over 16 years. The last 25 years have seen a large expansion of output from Pilbara to feed the steel industries of Korea and Taiwan. To service this industry there are today some 1150 km of track.

The Hamersley Railway was begun in June 1965 and construction was very rapid, reaching the first objective, Mount Tom Price, 288 km (179 miles) from Dampier in July 1966. Mount Tom Price rises a little over 700 m (2300 ft) above sea level. Today the terminus at Paraburdoo, reached in 1972, is a further 100 km (62 miles) on, at an altitude of about 400 m (1320 ft). Construction of the Mount Newman Railway, the longest of them all at 427 km (265 miles), was completed in even less time and was in operation 18 months after the contract was awarded.

103

LEFT Locomotives are scheduled for a visit to the heavy maintenance area after clocking up 30,000 km (18,600 miles). This picture shows one of the latest models, the Alco C-636R Rebuild (left) which features electronic control and monitoring and in-built load testing.

In recent years it has been recognized that much useful information has been obtained from the mining lines. The Australians have introduced science into the empirical world of high tonnage, while the North Americans are seeking big financial gains through tight control based on dedicated radio data links. The two extremes get together through the International Heavy Haul Association, IHHA, which was incorporated in September 1986. The qualification for membership is that member railways must operate trains of a minimum of 5000 tonnes with axleloads of over 21 tonnes, and move in excess of 20 million gross tonnes per year.

BELOW A large iron-ore carrier, berthing at East Inter-course Island, Port of Dampier, soon to accept its mineral cargo from a Hamersley iron train.

LOCOMOTIVES

A fleet of 47 3600hp diesel-electric locomotives provide the motive power for the Hamersley. Most were built in Australia under licence from American or Canadian companies, all but five having General Electric 16-cylinder engines. The remainder have General Motors engines, installed by Clyde Industries, Adelaide. Until 1985, trains consisted of 180 wagons, each weighing about 20 tonnes and carrying 100 tonnes of ore – a gross weight of 21,000 tonnes (20,625 tons) with an overall length of just over 1.7 km (1.1 mile). Experiments were then carried out with trains of 210 wagons weighing 25,000 tonnes (24,555 tons) with an overall length of 2 km (1.25 miles). These are the world's heaviest trains running with head-end power, that is with no helper locomotives along the train or at the rear.

Usually three locomotives haul the trains, which of course run back empty to the mines. In this direction they have to negotiate gradients as steep as 2 per cent (1 in 50) and even with three powerful locomotives hauling the 4200-tonne (4125-ton) train the speed falls to less than 20 km/h (12 mph). As mentioned in the first part of this chapter, the handling of these very long and heavy trains requires a great deal of skill, and today drivers are trained on an electronic simulator. Such training reveals the pitfalls that can be met on the road, and which have to be avoided if there are to be no expensive accidents.

HAMERSLEY RAILWAY (Australia)	
TRAFFIC:	Iron ore
Gauge:	Standard
Length of haul:	383 km (238 miles)
Max train weight:	25000 tonnes (24555 tons)
Locomotives per train:	6 (3 head end – 3 banking)
Speed on 1 in 140 gradient:	33–35 km/hr (20–22 mph)
TRACTION:	Diesel-electric locomotives
Types:	5 Clyde-GM – 3600 hp
	42 Comeng-Alco – 3600 hp
Wheel arrangement:	Co-Co
TRACK TYPE:	American standard
Weight of rails:	68 kg/m (137 lb/yd)
Sleepers (Ties):	Concrete
CIRCUIT TIME:	33 hours

GROUND CONTROL

The main control centre for the operation is at Seven Mile Yard, 11.2 km (7 miles) south of the port of Dampier. There a visual track diagram shows the location of all trains, and the condition of all signals and controlled points (switches). Taped radio telephone communication is maintained with train crews who can alert Control if there is any untoward incident which may affect the running of that or any other train. The whole area is subject to extreme weather conditions, and weather stations keep a constant watch for cyclones, which bring torrential rain with wind speeds up to 210 km/h (130 mph). The Hamersley aims to shut down about 12 hours ahead of any hurricane and when one is expected, train crews are collected and flown home to their bases, everyone remaining indoors until the danger has passed. Before operation can recommence, the line is inspected from the air and the track before trains are allowed to move again. Normally the railway operates every day except Christmas.

MAXIMIZING EFFICIENCY

The summit of the line is at Wombat Junction, 284 km (176 miles) from Dampier. From there to Paraburdoo the line falls on a continuous gradient of 0.417 per cent (1 in 140). Because loaded trains have to negotiate this gradient for 100 km (62 miles), three additional helper locomotives are employed to bank the train from the rear. All six locomotives must work on full power for three hours continuously to achieve a speed of 33-35 km/h (20-22 mph) with a train of 25,000 tonnes (24,555 tons).

To carry this very heavy traffic the permanent way (track and track bed) has to be to very high standards of construction and maintenance. It uses North American standard rails weighing 68 kg/m (137 lb/yard) — 55-58 kg/m is normal for European main lines — and concrete has replaced hardwood for the sleepers (ties). The aim is to maintain a time of 33 hours for the circuit Seven Mile Yard-Paraburdoo-Dampier-Seven Mile Yard with the heaviest train. In recent years the permanent way has been progressively improved with deeper ballasting, curve realignment, and improved points and crossings.

An important factor in maintaining the schedule is the speed of loading and unloading at the mines and the port with sophisticated mechanical handling. Loading times can vary from 1½ hours (lumps) to 5½ hours (fines), and if a certain time is exceeded the last few wagons may be left unloaded to minimize late running.

ROUTE OF THE HAMERSLEY RAILWAY

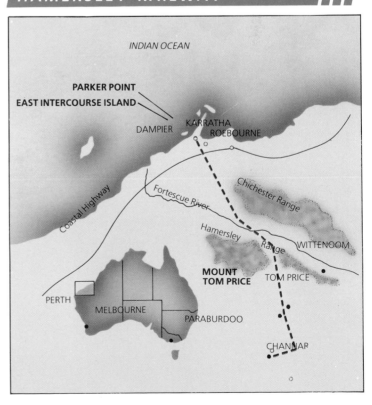

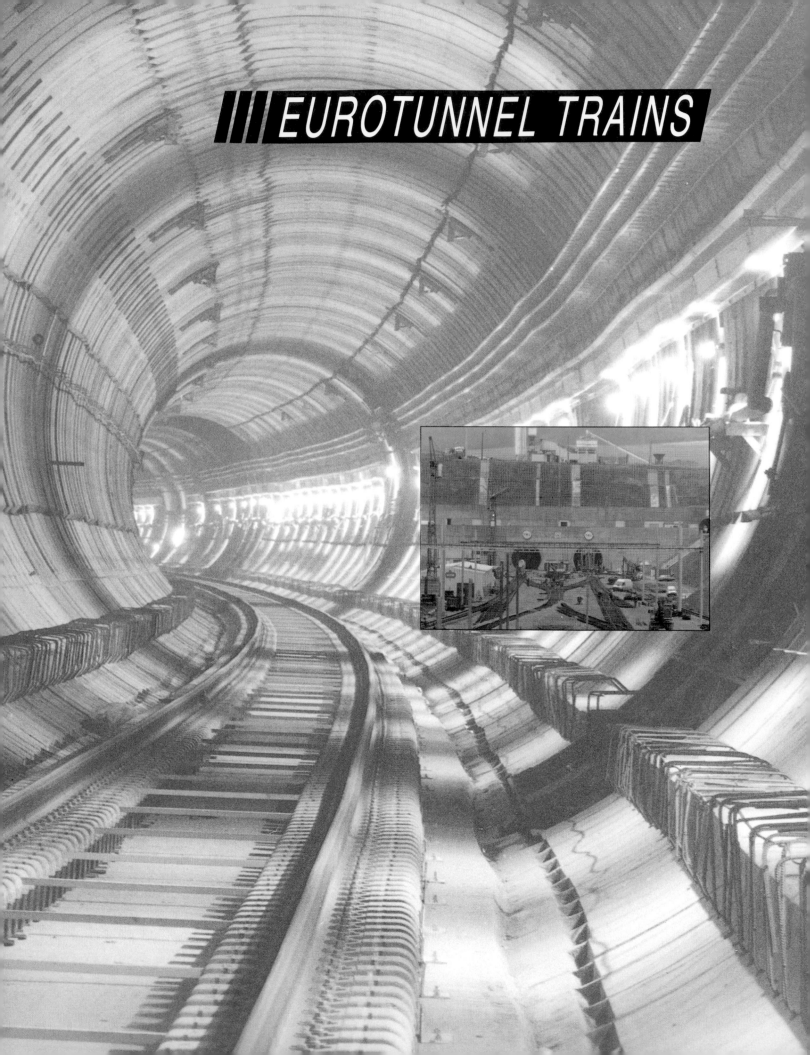

EUROTUNNEL TRAINS

THE CHANNEL TUNNEL LINK

The Channel Tunnel is one of the most exciting projects of the century and needs a book on its own to tell the story of its design, construction and operation. Yet the popular view of the Tunnel is that it exists solely as a transporter of cars and lorries to and from the Continent of Europe and will largely replace the existing ferries. In fact the Tunnel has a far wider purpose and will connect England, Scotland and Wales into the total land transport system of Europe. To quote Eurotunnel:

"The Channel Tunnel will be a railway system connecting terminals near Folkestone and Calais through bored one-way tunnels generally between 25 and 45 metres (82 and 148 feet) below the sea bed. The system will carry four main types of traffic:
1. cars and coaches in passenger shuttles,
2. heavy goods vehicles (HGVs) in freight shuttles, both operated by Eurotunnel,
3. through passenger trains,
4. through freight trains, both operated by the national railways."

For the first time Britain's railways will be physically connected with the railway system of the European Continent.

BACKGROUND

The idea of a tunnel under the English Channel has been mooted a number of times in the last 150 years.

But it was not until 1972, after many plans and reappraisals, that the British and French Governments decided detailed studies could proceed with a view to a final decision to start in 1973, with completion of the tunnel and commencement of operation in the winter of 1979-80. A new international airport on Maplin Sands, which would be served by a railway, was also to be built. Some preliminary work had been done on both projects when the British Labour Government decided unilaterally at the end of 1974 to ditch all of its agreements. The Tunnel, together with the proposed airport on Maplin Sands, was again put on ice. The French Government was livid, and work continued on the French side for some while afterwards.

But the Tunnel did not die. In 1978 British Railways advocated a single-track, no frills, rail-only tunnel which later gained the support of the French railway, SNCF. A single-track tunnel, constructed to the international loading gauge, would have been capable of becoming part of possible future developments. Again there were several rival proposals, including three for bridges. By 1980, some ten major appraisals had been completed but the scheme which at last bore fruit has two one-way tunnels, running parallel to a service tunnel, with a total length of 50 km (31 miles). As a matter of interest, the Japanese Seikan rail tunnel linking Honshu with Hokkaido is 53.83 km (33.45 miles) long but passes under a sea channel, the Tsuguru straits, only 23 km (12¼ miles) wide compared to the 36.6 km (22¾ miles) of Channel that separate France and England.

THE CHANNEL TUNNEL

Twin circular running tunnels with an internal diameter of 7.6 m (25 ft) have been completed, connected by a central 4.8 m (15 ft 9 in) diameter service tunnel. There are two undersea crossovers between the two running tunnels at approximately 16 km (10 miles) from each tunnel portal. The two road/rail terminals at Cheriton and Coquelles are connected to their respective motorway and national rail systems.

OPPOSITE **Channel Tunnel under construction from the French side.**

THE PASSENGER SHUTTLES

These trains will carry cars (automobiles), coaches (buses), minibuses and caravans (trailers and campers) and their passengers between the terminals at Cheriton (Folkestone) and Coquelles (Calais). Motor cars will be accommodated in double-deck tourist wagons. Larger vans and coaches will be conveyed in single-deck tourist vehicles.

THE SHUTTLE LOCOMOTIVES

Each shuttle will have a locomotive at each end of a train of 28 vehicles. For the time being the maximum speed will be limited to 130 km/h (80 mph). In order to negotiate the fairly steep gradients of 1.1 per cent (1 in 91) at each end of the tunnel, the pair of locomotives will develop some 11,200kW. Should one locomotive fail the other has to be capable of propelling the complete train to the most convenient terminal. In order to meet the normal operating requirements, it was clear at an early stage

CHANNEL TUNNEL TRAINS

Four main types of train are planned:

(i) **Passenger vehicle shuttle trains** Owned and operated by Eurotunnel, these will run between the two Tunnel terminals at Cheriton (Folkestone) and Coquelles (Calais). The trains will consist of 28 vehicles in semi-permanently coupled rakes with a special locomotive at each end. The journey time from terminal to terminal will be about 35 minutes, and for the time being they will reach a speed of 130 km/h (80 mph) en route.

(ii) **Freight shuttles** Owned and operated by Eurotunnel, these will also run only between the two terminals. They will have "open-sided" vehicles, and lorry crews will be accommodated in a separate passenger vehicle at the front of the train. A locomotive of the same type as for the passenger shuttles will be coupled at each end.

(iii) **Through passenger rail services** These are of three distinct types:

(a) **High-speed passenger trains** These are the Trans-Manche Super Trains – TMSTs.

They are jointly owned by BR, SNCB (Belgian Railways) and SNCF. They are a development of the French TGVs and will be the "Inter-Capital Super Trains" (ICSTs). Initially they will operate between the new terminal in London (Waterloo), Paris and Brussels.

(b) **North-of-London trains** These are similar to the TMSTs. They were authorized in December 1991 and will be owned by BR. They will operate between cities in the northern part of Britain and Continental destinations.

(c) **Night trains** of special locomotive-hauled sleeping cars.

(iv) **International freight trains** These will operate between various centres in Britain and the Continent with existing and new rolling stock. Continental freight rolling stock in most cases can operate over most main routes in Britain.

These last two will be hauled at least as far as Calais by a new design of dual-voltage electric locomotive, owned and operated by BR and SNCF, and designated Class 92.

OPPOSITE Designer's drawing of passenger vehicle shuttle locomotive.

BELOW Double-decker passenger vehicle shuttle car under construction.

that a total of 12 driven axles would be necessary. The emergency requirement could be met by a locomotive with six driven axles, so the neatest solution was to have a 5.6 MW Bo-Bo-Bo locomotive at each end of the train, the rear locomotive being controlled from the one at the front of the train. Three four-axle bogies enable the locomotives to easily negotiate the sharp curves at each of the two terminals.

A vital requirement is that the locomotives be powerful, safe and reliable machines entirely suited to the special demands of the environment of the Channel Tunnel. They have a number of special features to meet the very exacting specification. All possible steps have been taken to ensure the highest degree of reliability — and ABB have a very special knowledge of tunnel operation on the Swiss Federal Railways. Railway authorities in Switzerland have for some time stipulated that equipment be "Simplon-proof" — a reference to the 20-km (12.4-mile) Simplon Tunnel, currently the longest in Europe — and ABB equipment has been specially developed to cope with tunnel conditions.

TECHNICAL DETAILS	
SYSTEM OPERATOR:	Eurotunnel
TYPE OF LOCOMOTIVE:	Single-phase ac
DESIGNATION:	Shuttle-train locomotive
YEAR OF COMMISSIONING:	1993
TRACTION SYSTEM:	25kV ac 50Hz overhead
GAUGE:	1435 mm (4 ft 8½ in)
WHEEL ARRANGEMENT:	Bo-Bo-Bo
WEIGHT IN RUNNING ORDER:	132 tonnes (291,010 lb)
ADHESIVE WEIGHT:	132 tonnes (291,010 lb)
NO. OF TRACTION MOTORS:	6
CONTINUOUS RATING:	5600kW
STARTING TRACTIVE EFFORT:	400 kN (89925 lb)
TRACTION MOTOR RATING:	950kW
MOTOR TYPE:	Asynchronous, squirrel-cage
MAX. SPEED:	175 km/h (109 mph)
LENGTH, BUFFER FACE TO COUPLER FACE:	22008 mm (72 ft 2½ in)
WIDTH OVER BODY:	2996 mm (9 ft 8¾ in)
HEIGHT OF BODY FROM RAIL:	4200 mm (13 ft 9¼ in)
DISTANCE BETWEEN BOGIE CENTRES:	6350 and 6350 mm (2 × 20 ft 10 in)
BOGIE WHEELBASE:	2800 mm (9 ft 2¼ in)
WHEEL DIAMETER:	1250 mm (4 ft 1¼ in)
DESIGN AND MANUFACTURE:	Euroshuttle Consortium Locos
LOCOMOTIVE BUILDER:	Brush Traction Limited
ELECTRICAL EQUIPMENT:	ABB Transportation Systems Ltd

OPPOSITE ABOVE **Mock-up of a driver's cab. A secondary set of driving controls is also provided at the rear for limited speed operation in case of emergency.**

OPPOSITE BELOW **Model of a shuttle locomotive. The wedge-shaped front and rear is effective in cutting down air resistance and drag respectively.**

IN CASE OF EMERGENCY...

The locomotives must be capable of safe operation in emergency and the following conditions have to be met:

1. In the event of one bogie set of equipment being inoperable, the locomotive must be able to re-start the train on the maximum gradient (1.1 per cent/1 in 91) and accelerate at 0.13 m/sec/sec (0.29 mph/sec).

2. If a complete locomotive fails, the remaining locomotive must be able to re-start the train on the maximum gradient and move the train to the terminal.

3. Should a shuttle train suffer a complete failure, a following shuttle train must be able to push the failed train out.

The locomotive's main driving cab is complemented at the rear by a secondary driving cab, from which the locomotive may be driven up to a maximum speed of 80 km/h (50 mph).

The electric power transmission equipment consists of three identical units per locomotive, each of which may operate entirely independently of the others. This means that a breakdown in one equipment will lead to a 16.7 per cent power reduction only, there being six such equipments per train.

The control equipment of the shuttle train is the latest in hi-tech. The three-phase drive technology has many advantages — motors with no commutators, no brushes, no slip rings, no uninsulated parts; the power inverter has no moving parts, no fuses; the power circuit has no contacts which have to be switched, vehicle reversing takes place without contacts, and changeover from motoring to electric braking is effected without contactors. Much of the wiring in the inverter circuitry is replaced by fibre-optics, which give a high degree of immunity from electrical and magnetic disturbances.

Apart from the two driving cabs on the locomotive, it is also possible to move a train from a position in the end loader wagons and even by remote control from a standing position beside the train. Speed is limited to 30 km/h (18.6 mph) and 4 km/h (2.5 mph) respectively in these modes. The driving compartments are air-conditioned, which will ensure a controlled temperature within ±1°C of the desired temperature irrespective of the wide variations of external temperature as the train enters and leaves the Tunnel. The driver will of course drive from the

leading cab, and the rear locomotive cab will be occupied by a "train captain" who will have at his disposal an array of visual-display units and instrumentation to provide him with a continuous flow of information on the status of the shuttle-wagons.

Some unusual features are being built into the locomotives to suit the Tunnel operation. The tourist wagons will have air-suspension and other features requiring a substantial air supply. This will be provided from the locomotives. The shuttle-wagons will also have air-conditioning and ventilation, lighting, and so on which will have a high power demand, all of which will come from the locomotives. Power for these services will be taken from a 1500V dc line running the entire length of the train.

During the course of the journey the train will pass through about six neutral sections where the overhead catenary will be dead. The approach to each section will have signalling devices to enable the traction power to be shut off and on again in a controlled manner. The same signals will be passed through to the wagons so that their electrical loads can be partly shed then re-applied

in a controlled manner to avoid overloading the 1500V dc system.

Automatic Train Protection (ATP) is being provided, with allowance for the possible future fitting of Automatic Train Operation (ATO) equipment. There will also be track-to-train radio, concession radio, a shuttle internal radio, and train communication and public address system equipment installed on the locomotives.

Considerable care is being taken to ensure that train drivers have the correct driving environment and that continuous tunnel driving does not pose any threat to their concentration and vigilance, hence the provision of ATP. The drivers' cabs will be well sealed to minimize pressure transients that will occur when travelling at speed through the Tunnel.

The shuttle locomotives will be powerful, sophisticated, safe, reliable machines specially designed and constructed to operate in the demanding environment of the Channel Tunnel. Microprocessor control is linked with a health-monitoring unit with video displays in the driver's cab.

THE VEHICLES

Four types of vehicles are being provided for the passenger shuttles: single- and double-deck end-loaders, double-deck auto-carrier Tourist Wagons, and single-deck coach and van Tourist Wagons. Very comprehensive trials with full-size mock-ups have been carried out to determine the best means of loading and unloading road vehicles, and the results have been used in the design of the terminal facilities and of the vehicles themselves.

In all but a few cases, drivers and passengers will remain in their cars during the journey of about 35 minutes. Motorcycles will be carried in a special section, and their riders will travel in passenger compartments. Separate arrangements are being made for the carriage of cycles and cyclists. Cars and other vehicles up to 1.85 m (6 ft) high, including roof racks, will travel in double-deck wagons; 126 of these are being built by Bombardier of Canada and its French subsidiary ANF-Industrie. They will normally make up half of a complete train. The other half will comprise single-deck vehicles for mini-buses and coaches; 126 of these are also being built by another Bombardier subsidiary, BN of Belgium.

There will be nine complete trains, each consisting of 30 vehicles, with a total length of 792 m (2598 ft): locomotive + loader + 12 carriers + 2 loaders + 12 carriers + loader + locomotive. The carrier wagons are semi-permanently coupled in sets of three, the outer wagon of each set being fitted with automatic couplers, as are the loaders. Apart from the 28 m (91 ft 10 in) long double-deck end loaders, all vehicles will be 26 m (85 ft 3½ in) long. The height of 5.6 m (18 ft 4½ in) is sufficient to

LEFT The control centre continuously monitors all movements between terminals, as well as keeping a constant watch on all internal tunnel services.

accommodate 4.2 m (13 ft 9¼ in) high coaches on the single-deck carriers (SDCs), and the internal width of 3.75 m (12 ft 3½ in) leaves sufficient room for a walkway on each side.

A single-deck loader (SDL) has three telescopic hoods which slide back to reveal the 18 m (59 ft) loading area. To bridge the gap between vehicle and platform, fold-down plates are employed similar to those which have been used successfully for many years on the Transalpine shuttles. At the outer end there is a small saloon, a crew room and three lavatories.

The double-deck loaders (DDLs) have 6 m (19 ft 8¼ in) sliding doors on each side at each end. Cars for the upper deck will use the door at the outer end, then drive up a fixed ramp to the adjacent wagons. Access to the lower deck is through the inner end-loading door, which will also be used by motorcyclists who will stow their machines in a compartment beneath the ramp. They will travel in a small saloon at the outer end of the upper deck, where lavatories and a crew compartment are also provided. Access to this area is by stairs at the extreme end of the vehicle, where there is also a gangway door for crew access to the adjacent locomotive.

The centre wagon of each set of three has stairs on one side, with a lavatory on each deck, one under and one over the 0.8 m (2 ft 7¾ in) wide stairs. The length

BELOW The single-deck vehicles will be used to transport coaches, vans and caravans, which need more headroom than can be provided in the double-deck vehicles.

113

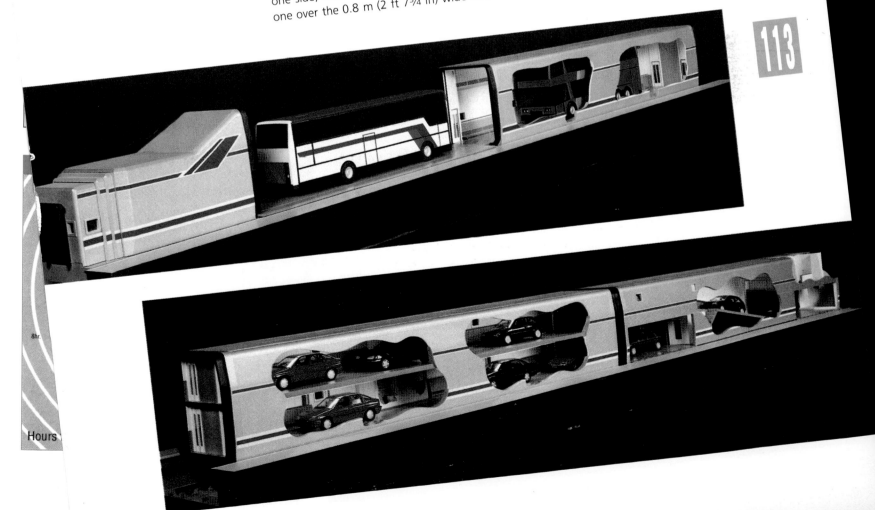

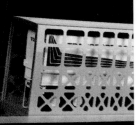

MLU
002

RAINS

The previous chapters have shown how railways of today are making use of high technology. But what about tomorrow? Where do railways go from here? What developments can improve the already good record of railways for mass public transport? The already substantial mileage of new railways in Europe and elsewhere will be extended. Already there are plans for a new line connecting Paris, Brussels and Cologne, with a connection to the French Channel Tunnel terminal and possibly branch to Amsterdam. There is a vision of a much wider European high-speed network — a vision which will employ modern technology for the trains, track, and signalling and control systems.

Already the technology of the existing French TGV trains is last generation. The new trains for the through services to the Channel Tunnel are being built with the latest in hi-tech. The use of on-board computers is now regarded as normal, and there is little doubt that as microprocessors become even more clever they will take on new and greater significance.

OPPOSITE **The Colorado Test Center is able to re-create actual running conditions on three different test tracks: 24 km (15 miles) of ac electrified track for main-line use); 16 km (10 miles) of track equipped with third-rail dc electrification; and a light-rail-type catenary .**

BELOW **The Association of American Railroads provides research and specialized test facilities at the Transportation Test Center in Pueblo, Colorado. Here, an Amtrak locomotive is evaluated on the roll dynamics unit.**

DEVELOPMENTS IN NORTH AMERICA

Some people seem to think that railways in the United States have not kept up with developments in Europe. Their apparent reluctance to "advance" results from special conditions, which will be explained. This too will change. In the 1980s, the American privately-owned freight railways were freed from many regulations that had prevented them from competing effectively with road transport. Mergers and reorganization aimed at the consumer, together with better use of existing resources, made money available for other developments. But these objectives depend critically on reliable locomotives.

During the next few years, the development of American locomotives will be heavily influenced by these issues. Manufacturers will be under severe pressure to improve reliability and maintainability, while reducing exhaust emissions without loss of efficiency. Three trends can now be identified as:

(i) the introduction of asynchronous three-phase electric traction motors

(ii) the expanding use of microprocessors for real-time diagnostic monitoring of a locomotive's condition

(iii) the role of federal and state agencies in formulating regulations for exhaust emissions standards, with which manufacturers must comply.

119

MICROPROCESSORS

Microprocessors have been used in locomotives for a number of reasons, a major one being their diagnostic application. Maintenance departments can anticipate and cure problems before actual failure occurs if an impending fault can be identified. Faults in operating systems can be monitored and reported, together with diagnostic help for a cure. Temperatures, pressures, fuel, lubricating oil and water supplies can all be monitored.

Locomotives can be equipped with on-board computers, while displays enable data to be read direct from the microprocessors. Data can also be transferred over a communications link to a remote place (maintenance depot) for action. Most of the monitored quantities will have operating limits; exceeding these will give a fault warning. If the quantity then returns within the limits, a "fault clear" or similar indication is given. If data on "faults" and "clears" is stored in the computer's memory, those annoying "intermittent" faults (which would otherwise go undetected) can be identified.

Locomotive operation and maintenance is being revolutionized through the microprocessor. As computers become smaller and even more powerful, advances in the design of operating systems will be a further aid to utilization and reliability.

ELECTRIC TRACTION MOTORS

Three-phase drives are now widely used in Europe, but there has been no significant application of them in North America for main-line railways. The benefits, which bear repeating here, include reduced maintenance because there are no commutators or brushes, which in turn eliminates the risk of flash-over and moisture-related earthing problems.

North American dc motor drives are nevertheless very reliable but represent an on-going cost. Integrating the complex power electronics and computers required to control ac traction motors into the locomotive, while maintaining and even improving already high reliability – and doing so at reasonable cost – requires some courage! The 1990s will see a new breed of high-power locomotives with ac traction drives on American railways. The first of four new generation 2835kW (3800hp) SD60MAC locomotives, developed jointly by Siemens and General Motors Locomotive Group, are already being tested on GMLC facilities. They will then go to the joint test ground of the Association of American Railroads (AAR) at Pueblo, Colorado, and are expected to enter service before the winter of 1992-3.

BELOW **The F69PH diesel-electric high-speed locomotive for Amtrak in the US features the latest AC three-phase technology.**

120

MINIMIZING POLLUTION

The control of exhaust emissions is in everybody's interest. In the United States the revisions to the 1990 Clean Air Act directed the American Environmental Protection Agency to issue new emissions regulations for new and re-engined locomotives. The Act allows states with problems of air pollution, such as California, to also impose limits on emissions from existing locomotives. Similar action is likely before long from the EEC.

Most of the above is not confined to the United States. Already diagnostic systems are in use in Europe, and reference has already been made to pre-journey checks by on-board computers in the chapter on high-speed trains. Even greater use of on-board computers is being made on the new breed of Trans-Manche Super Trains for the Channel Tunnel.

EQUIPMENT FOR DIESEL-ELECTRIC ROLLING STOCK WITH AC THREE-PHASE TECHNOLOGY

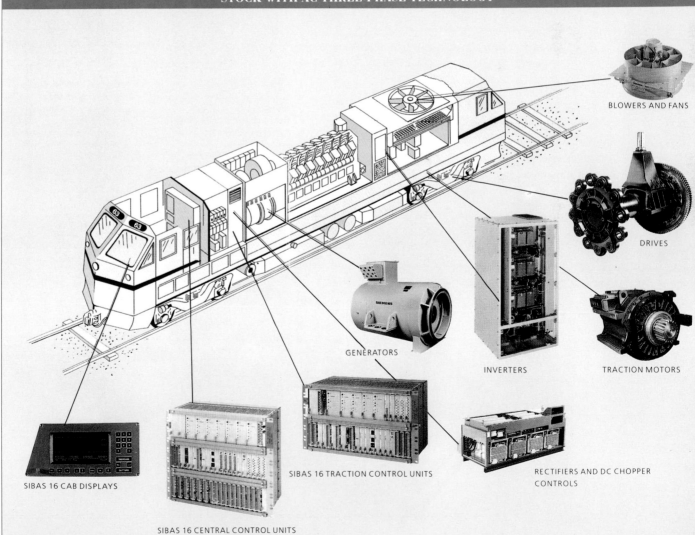

BLOWERS AND FANS

DRIVES

TRACTION MOTORS

INVERTERS

RECTIFIERS AND DC CHOPPER CONTROLS

GENERATORS

SIBAS 16 TRACTION CONTROL UNITS

SIBAS 16 CAB DISPLAYS

SIBAS 16 CENTRAL CONTROL UNITS

PASSENGER COMFORT

Railways have to compete effectively with road and air transport. To win traffic from either, they must offer something the competition does not. Very fast city-centre to city-centre travel has been a feature of rail for at least the last decade, and has steadily attracted more and more passengers.

Apart from speed, railways can offer very comfortable travel in relatively quiet air-conditioned vehicles. It used to be said that British railways could not justify the cost of air-conditioning because of the relatively equable climate. That may once have been true financially, but it is no longer the case because the level of sound and heat insulation now expected can be obtained only with a sealed vehicle – with fixed windows and the very minimum of well-fitting doors. This requires air-conditioning.

Comfortable seating, comfortable environment, good decor and a good ride are all built into today's vehicles. But, as we have seen, high speed brings a special factor into play, and that is comfort in curves. New single-purpose high-speed lines are laid out with due regard to comfort in curves and as far as possible large radius, canted curves are the norm. But what about existing lines? Where passenger and freight trains share a common route the question of curvature has to be very carefully considered.

For comfort on winding routes the tilting train is an answer. But, as we have seen, in Italy nausea became a problem and had to be addressed. More tilting trains will probably be used, but only where curves are very severe and the traffic warrants high speed over such routes. The additional complexity is expensive to instal and maintain.

Comfortable ride is another factor, determined by the train's suspension. Air secondary springing is now well established. Air-bag manufacturing is well understood and air-springs are reliable. There will be some extension of air suspensions to very high-speed trains, in Germany in particular. But what about "active" suspensions?

So-called active systems were discussed in the chapter on tilting trains. Present vehicle suspensions may be described as "passive" – they react after something happens. Rail vehicle suspension in particular is a good example of the engineer's art. The designer has to reconcile a number of conflicting requirements to cope with an unpredictable and changing series of demands. The primary aim is to cushion the passenger from the effects of irregularities in the track. To achieve this aim the designer uses primary and secondary suspensions, with various combinations of springs and dampers (a car's primary springing is its rubber tyres!).

The designer tries to produce a vehicle body that takes a level path through space and for the passengers to be unaware, as far as possible, of sharp disturbances of a relatively high frequency. These must be absorbed by the

OPPOSITE ABOVE Car body tilt technology has been developed for increased passenger comfort in curves. It has been found that the optimal compensation for lateral acceleration is 80 per cent, which is achieved at tilting angles up to a maximum of 8 degrees.

OPPOSITE BELOW Increasingly high speeds on new-generation trains have meant a greater concentration on passenger safety and comfort. At the Railway Technical Research Institute in Japan, the effects of acceleration are assessed in a test unit.

122

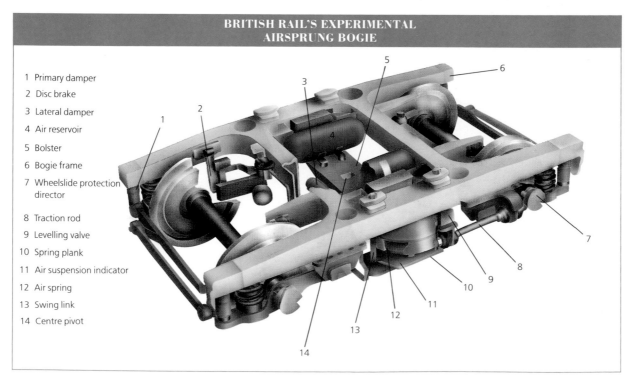

BRITISH RAIL'S EXPERIMENTAL AIRSPRUNG BOGIE

1 Primary damper
2 Disc brake
3 Lateral damper
4 Air reservoir
5 Bolster
6 Bogie frame
7 Wheelslide protection director
8 Traction rod
9 Levelling valve
10 Spring plank
11 Air suspension indicator
12 Air spring
13 Swing link
14 Centre pivot

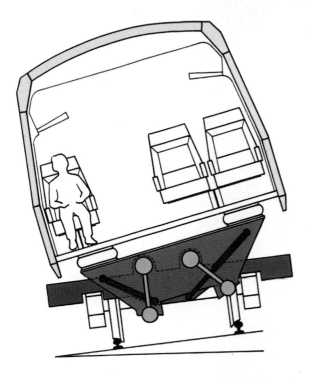

NEW TRANSPORT SYSTEMS

As long ago as 1966, the British Institution of Mechanical Engineers in London organized a conference with the title "Guided Land Transport". It is interesting, 25 years on, to see what the conference identified as the major developments in trains leading up to the millennium.

(a) Pneumatic-tyred trains of the Paris Metro type or variants.

(b) Monorails

(c) Guided air-cushion vehicles

(d) Magnetic suspension – Maglev.

The first three have already been discussed, so it is appropriate here to have a brief look at Maglev because it is considered by some, particularly the Japanese, to be the replacement for conventional high-speed railways in the next century.

MAGLEV

The German high-speed system, known as Transrapid 06, was to have been a contender for one of the lines now operated as a Neubahnstrecke. The German Transport Ministry was not convinced that Maglev had demonstrated the level of safety necessary for a public transport system. Also, because it had to be carried on elevated concrete guideways, it was very far from environmentally friendly, so necessary in modern Germany.

The Japanese have a test track at Miyazaku and seemed to be having success. They have achieved a speed of 515 km/h (320 mph) while unmanned, and 407 km/h (253 mph) manned. Unfortunately in November 1991 a serious fire, apparently starting in the rubber-tyred emergency wheels, damaged the vehicle badly. The Japanese are still pinning their faith on Maglev as a replacement for the Shinkansens when they pass their usefulness in the early part of the next century.

The low-speed installation, used as a people-mover between Birmingham International Airport and the adjacent British Rail station, has been operating well since 1984. There are two independent tracks, and normally one unmanned car operates on each under automatic control from a computer at the airport end. A third car is kept as a spare for maintenance and so on.

It is an eerie experience riding for the first time when the warning sounds and the doors close, to feel the vehicle rise some 15 mm then move off entirely automatically. There is a pronounced hum from the electronics. The tight first curve is negotiated slowly, the pitch of the electronic hum changes, and the vehicle accelerates to its cruising speed of about 40 km/h (25 mph). As the car approaches the airport terminal, the electronic hum changes down and the speed is reduced to negotiate the second sharp curve. The stop at the platform is smooth.

suspension. But there are also gentle, low-frequency disturbances. A slight dip in the track is a case in point. Here it is desirable for the coach body to follow the path of the bogie, or the body would tend to bounce on the secondary springs, which is uncomfortable. The aim of the vehicle designer must be to minimize the effect on the vehicle body of the "bumps" in the track, and at the same time minimize the displacement of the body relative to the bogie. Reducing the latter accentuates the former!

An active suspension has some external element to augment the effect of the secondary suspension. Much of the compromise of the passive suspension can be bypassed, yet, should the active element fail, the bogie must still have an acceptable ride. Electronic control can measure the parameters, and where there are conflicting demands filter out the information which is not relevant to particular conditions. With very high-speed travel, active suspension makes a lot of sense and here is an area where there is development potential for the future.

123

124

The car settles down on to the track and the doors open to allow the passengers out.

Other modern airports have not so far been attracted to Maglev, instead preferring the slightly less complex but well-developed Westinghouse (or similar) people-mover system used widely in the United States. This runs on a concrete guideway employing rubber tyres and conventional dc motors. Installations in Britain include those at Gatwick and Stanstead airports.

THE FUTURE

To revert to the predictions of the 1966 conference, we can see that little has changed. Of the four non-conventional systems quoted, the use of rubber tyres has had limited success and even the Paris Metro has only converted a few of its lines. Although the systems are capable of fast acceleration, the wear on the rubber tyres has always been an on-going cost, and there is the problem of rubber being deposited on the guideways. Remote from French influence there has been little interest.

Monorails also enjoy a very limited success. Those that have been successful are not true monorails but have a single beam with one carrying and two guide tracks, and a multiplicity of rubber tyres. The same consideration of tyre wear applies equally. Monorails are popular for pleasure parks where a scenic ride is needed, or they can be incorporated into the urban scene where there are space limitations.

Air-cushion vehicles have been tried and abandoned, for the moment anyway. Even the hovercraft has had a very limited application. Its main use has been for light transport over relatively difficult — mainly swampy or sandy — terrain.

Maglev is still in the development stage, particularly for high-speed transport. Permanent magnets have not been used for support as envisaged. So, as with air-cushion vehicles, power has to be expended to support the vehicles at the appropriate closely-controlled height above the guideways, using some form of computer control to maintain the vehicle within the very tight limits.

The main area for development would seem the extension of high-speed conventional railways. Already speeds in the 300-320 km/h (185-200 mph) range are safe and practical. Trains will be operating at those speeds very soon on new purpose-built lines in Europe and elsewhere. The use of microprocessors is already well-established, and they will have an even greater part to play in the next decade. Tilting trains have a place too to reduce journey times on existing routes where there are many curves.

Radio control has not been mentioned so far. Radio control of locomotives has been employed for special purposes for many years. Radio-controlled signalling systems are now practical but security must be absolute, and inductive systems are more likely to be extended in the future. Radio communication between trains and ground stations is now part of the luxury train scene and will undoubtedly come into more general use in the near future. Radio communication between driver and ground control is now already being extended. It has been employed on the major railroads in the United States for a good many years.

Driverless trains, as we have seen, are practical, but the totally unmanned train is not so common. Because of the ever-present problem of vandalism, railway companies are reluctant to have no staff at all on trains. Totally safe operation under computer control is practical without train staff. But passengers need to feel secure, and the presence of somebody "in authority" on the trains lends some comfort, and may act as a deterrent to would-be vandals. Scanning of station platforms by video cameras is now common, and developments in visual communications will improve security.

ELECTRIFICATION

There is little doubt that we shall see much more electrification. It has always made sense to site power stations near to the sources of fuel, and these sites do not have to be near cities. Power distribution networks are well developed, and railways can and do tap into the distribution networks where they need the power.

We are used to high-voltage alternating current taken from overhead contact wires, and the normal voltage today is 25,000 volts. For the future there could be a case for reverting to direct current at around 12,000 volts. With the development of power electronic devices, it is no longer necessary to use direct current motors. The conversion from direct to variable-frequency alternating current is now practical and widely employed.

High-voltage direct current has attractions in a number of ways. Electromagnetic interference from the contact wires is largely eliminated, and losses in transmission are less. The electrical power link between England and France uses direct current because losses in an alternating current link would be untenable.

We have not touched urban transport, in which high technology will also play a major part in the future. This is a subject on its own. The major railway systems are all in intensely competitive situations today, and their success or otherwise is linked to the ability to make effective use of the new technology as it develops.

MAGLEV: ENGINEERING'S OPTIMISM

125

To quote from the Institution of Mechanical Engineers conference again, the introduction to the subject of Magnetic Suspension contains the following:

Tracked transport by magnetic suspension is now a practical proposition for slow as well as highest speeds. Vehicles float with clearance of up to an inch on a magnetic field requiring no power expenditure, and hence without noise and the need for maintenance. Development is now at the man-carrying model stage, including propulsion-braking by simple dc linear motor that uses the track permanent field for excitation.

This (paper) summarises nine years of development into what is considered to be their (massive permanent magnets') largest and most important application, land transport, both guided and random-travel. . . . The objective is the magnetic suspension of simple raft-like vehicles. They float up to an inch above a track with a permanent field which also provides the medium for ideal weightless springing, shock-absorbing and simple linear propulsion. . . . All this work has reached the stage at which the basic problems appear to be solved, but much engineering remains to be done.

This all sounded very simple and attractive, but how much engineering really needed to be done is perhaps illustrated by the fact that today, 25 years after the above was written, there is one low-speed system operating in Britain at Birmingham Airport, one in Germany, and very high-speed systems still under development in Germany and Japan.

GLOSSARY OF ABBREVIATIONS

ABB Asea Brown Boveri (grouping of ASEA, Sweden & Brown Boveri Company, Switzerland)

AEI Associated Electrical Industries – taken over by GEC-Alsthom, Britain

APT Advanced Passenger Train (BR)

ASEA Swedish General Electric Company (see ABB)

ATC Automatic Train Control

ATO Automatic Train Operation

ATP Automatic Train Protection

AWS Automatic Warning System

BBC Brown Boveri Company (see ABB)

Bo-Bo Powered vehicle with two independent 2-axle bogies; all axles driven by separate motors

BR British Railways

BTH British Thompson-Houston – taken over by GEC-Alsthom

CFF Chemin de Fer Fédéreaux – Swiss Federal Railways (also SBB)

Co-Co Powered vehicle with two independent 3-axle bogies; all axles driven by separate motors

Comeng Commonwealth Engineering Co, Australia (formerly)

CTC Centralized Train Control, Coded track circuits

CV Continental horsepower = 736 watts

CWR Continuously welded rail

DB Deutsche Bundesbahn – German Federal Railways

DLR Docklands Light Railway (London)

DMC Driving motor car

DTC Driving trailer car (sometimes Control Trailer)

DVT Driving van trailer

EEC European Economic Community

EECo English Electric Company (taken over by GEC Alsthom)

FS Ferrovie dello Stato – Italian State Railways

hp Imperial horsepower = 746 watts

HST High-speed train

Hz Herz – cycles per second

IC InterCity

IHHA International Heavy Haul Association

JNR Japanese National Railways

HGV Heavy goods vehicle (road)

km Kilometre (1 km = 0.621 mile)

km/h Kilometres per hour (1 km/h = 0.621 mph)

kN Kilo Newton (1 kN = 224.8lb force approx)

kV Kilovolts – thousandths of volts

kVA Kilovolt-amperes

kW Kilowatts (1 kW = 1000 Watts)

LCD Liquid crystal device

LGV Ligne grande vitesse – French high-speed line

LIM Linear induction motor

LRT Light rapid transit

LV Low voltage

Maglev Magnetic Levitation

mph Miles per hour (1 mph = 1.609 km/h)

MW Megawatts (1 MW = 1 million Watts)

NBS Neubaustrecke – Germany – new high-speed line

NDMC Non-driving motor car

NSW New South Wales (Australia)

OPO One person operation

RER Reseau Express Regional – Paris

RTG Rame Turbine à Gaz – SNCF Gas Turbine railcars

SAR South African Railways

SBB Schweizerische Bundesbahnen – Swiss Federal Railways (CFF)

Shinkansen New railway – Japan

SJ Statens Jarnvager – Swedish State Railways

SNCB Société National Chemin de Fer Belgique – Belgian Railways

SNCF Société National de Chemin de Fer – French Railways

SRAWS Signal Repeating Automatic Warning System (BR)

TC Trailer car

TDM Time divison multiplex

TGV Train à Grande Vitesse – French high-speed train

TMST Trans Manche Super Train – (BR – SNCB – SNCF)

UTDC Urban Transit Development Corporation (Canada)

VAL Véhicule Automatique Légère – France, Matra

VDU Visual display unit

XPT Express Passenger Train (Australia)

INDEX

PICTURE CREDITS

L = left; r = right; M = middle; T = top; B = bottom; F = far

ABB Trazione: 65, 67. AEG: 8L, 50, 88. BC Transit: 8FL, 75, 76, 77, 78, 79, 81. Bertin & Cie: 86 (inset), 93. British Rail: 46B, 47. BZA München: 51M (photo: Krupp), 52 (photo: Schneider). Central Japan Railway Company: 5, 22, 23, 28, 29, 30, 31, 32–3, 34, 35. The Channel Tunnel Group: 9R, 21, 106, 108, 109, 111, 112, 113, 114. John Cormack: 36 (inset), 42. Design Triangle: 86, 94, 95. Docklands Light Railway: 82, 84, 85. Fiat Ferroviaria: 58, 59, 60, 61, 62, 63, 123T. French Railways (Société National de Chemin de Fer): 6FL, 10, 11, 12, 12–13, 14, 15, 16, 17, 18, 19, 20. GEC Alsthom: 44B, 83, 98–9. German Federal Railways (Deutsche Bundesbahn): 7R, 48 (inset), 49, 51T, 54–5, 56, 57. Hamersley Iron Railway: 8–9, 96, 100–1, 102–3, 104. Japan Monorail Association: 91. Jones Garrard: 11b. London Illustrated News: 89. C. J. Marsden: 7FR, 37, 39, 40, 44T, 46T, 47 (inset), 64. Missabe Range Railway Company: 97. Mitsubishi Electric: 9FR, 118, 124. Tony Nichols: 6–7, 43. Railway Technical Research Institute, Japan: 123. Siemens: 120, 121. TNT Harbourlink: 87. Tokyu Car Corporation: 6L, 26–7. Transport en Commun de la Communauté Urbaine de Lille (TCC): 68, 69, 70, 71, 72, 73, 74. Transportation Test Center, Colorado: 118 (inset), 119. Wuppertaler Stadtwerke AG: 92.